WRITERS AND THEIR WORK

ISOBEL ARMSTRONG
General Editor

BRYAN LOUGHREY
Advisory Editor

ANTHONY TROLLOPE

ANTHONY TROLLOPE
a study by Sir Leslie Ward ('Spy') of 1873
by courtesy of the National Portrait Gallery, London

ANTHONY TROLLOPE

Andrew Sanders

NORTHCOTE

BRITISH COUNCIL

ATLANTIC
PUBLISHERS & DISTRIBUTORS (P) LTD

This edition is published by
ATLANTIC
PUBLISHERS & DISTRIBUTORS (P) LTD
7/22, Ansari Road, Darya Ganj, New Delhi-110 002
Tel: 40775252, 23273880, 23275880, 23280451; Fax: +91-11-23285873
E-mail: orders@atlanticbooks.com; Web: www.atlanticbooks.com

By arrangement with
Northcote House Publishers Ltd
Horndon House, Horndon, Tavistock, Devon, PL19 9NQ,
United Kingdom. (T)+44(0)1822 810066; (F)+44(0)1822 810034
(E) northcote.house@virgin.net and (W) www.northcotehouse.co.uk
The *Writers and their Work* series is published in association with
the British Council.

First Indian Reprint 2010
First published in 1998 by Northcote House Publishers Ltd

ISBN 978-81-269-1301-5

British Library Cataloguing-in-Publication Data
A catalogue record for this book is available from the British Library

Typeset by PDQ Typesetting, Newcastle-under-Lyme
Printed in India at Nice Printing Press, A-33/3A, Site-IV,
Industrial Area, Sahibabad, Ghaziabad, U.P.

Contents

Acknowledgements

My thanks are due to three Trollopians who directly influenced what I have written. Roy Foster's enthusiasm helped me to appreciate the political acuteness of Trollope's fiction when we jointly taught the Victorian MA at Birkbeck College; John Sutherland's sharp introductions and astute annotations to the many editions of Trollope that he has prepared opened my mind to many fresh aspects of the fiction; finally, Reg Terry's pressing invitation to me to contribute to his Oxford Author Companion to *Anthony Trollope* happily obliged me to look closely both at aspects of Trollope's life and work and at generations of Trollope scholarship.

Biographical Outline

1815 24 April: Anthony Trollope born at Keppel Street, London. 18 June: final defeat of Napoleon at Waterloo. The Trollope family move to Harrow.

1823 Trollope begins his formal education as a day boy at Harrow School.

1825 Trollope sent to a private school in Sunbury.

1827 Trollope enters Winchester College. Frances Trollope embarks on her American adventure.

1831 Trollope moves back to Harrow School from Winchester.

1832 Frances Trollope publishes *Domestic Manners of the Americans* followed by her first novel, *The Refugee in America*. June: passage of the Reform Bill in Parliament.

1833 John Keblé's Assize sermon at Oxford. Beginning of Oxford Movement.

1834 April: Trollope family moves to Bruges. November: Trollope appointed to a clerkship in the General Post Office.

1837 Accession of Queen Victoria.

1840 Penny Post established.

1841 July: Trollope appointed to a clerkship in the Central District of the Post Office in Ireland. September: Trollope moves to Banagher, Co. Cork.

1844 June: Trollope marries Rose Heseltine.

1845 Irish Potato Famine.

1846 Birth of first son, Henry Merivale Trollope ('Harry').

1847 Trollope's first novel, *The Macdermots of Ballycloran*, published. Birth of second son, Frederic James Anthony Trollope ('Fred').

1851 Great Exhibition. August: Trollope sent to reorganize postal deliveries in the south-west of England. November: Trollope suggests introduction of pillar boxes in Jersey.

1852 May: Trollope visits Salisbury and 'conceives' story of *The Warden*.

1853 Northcote–Trevelyan Report calls for reform of the Civil Service. Trollope appointed acting surveyor for Northern district of Ireland.

1854 Crimean War.

1855 Trollope's fourth novel, *The Warden*, published.

1857 *Barchester Towers* published.

1858 February: Trollope sent on postal mission to Egypt. November: Trollope sent on postal mission to West Indies.

1859 Palmerston becomes Liberal Prime Minister (1859–65). Trollope's first visit to the United States. Summer: Trollope appointed Surveyor of Eastern District of England and settles in Waltham Cross.

1860 *Framley Parsonage* serialized in the *Cornhill Magazine* (Jan. 1860–June 1861). October: visits mother and brother in Florence. Meets Kate Field.

1861 American Civil War (1861–5). August: extended visit to United States on Post Office business. *Orley Farm* serialized in monthly parts (Mar. 1861–Oct. 1862).

1862 Spring: returns from United States. *The Small House at Allington* serialized in the *Cornhill Magazine* (Sept. 1862–April. 1864).

1863 October: death of Frances Trollope (buried in Florence). December: Death of Thackeray.

1864 *Can You Forgive Her?* (first Palliser novel) serialized in monthly parts (Jan. 1864–Aug. 1865).

1866 *The Last Chronicle of Barset* (final Barchester novel) serialized in weekly parts (Dec. 1866–July 1867).

1867 October: Trollope resigns from the Post Office and becomes Editor of *Saint Pauls Magazine*.

1868 March: sent to United States to negotiate postal convention. November: stands unsuccessfully as Liberal candidate at Beverley.

1870 Trollope retires from editorship of *Saint Pauls Magazine*.

1871 The Trollopes give up their house at Waltham Cross (April) and embark on an extended visit to Australia and New Zealand (May 1871–Oct. 1872).

1872 December: the Trollopes return to Britain via the United States. They settle in Montagu Square.

1874 *The Way We Live Now* serialized in monthly parts (Feb. 1874–Sept. 1875).

1875 February: Trollope embarks for second visit to Australia. October: On the return voyage begins work on *An Autobiography.*

1876 Completes *An Autobiography* (published posthumously in 1883). Trollope finishes the last Palliser novel, *The Duke's Children* (serialized Oct. 1879–July 1880).

1877 June: embarks for visit to South Africa. December: returns to Britain.

1878 June–July: Trollope visits Iceland.

1879 Publication of Trollope's study, *Thackeray.*

1880 July: the Trollopes move to South Harting, Sussex.

1882 May and August: Trollope revisits Ireland twice to collect material for *The Land-Leaguers,* his forty-seventh novel. 6 December: Trollope dies in London and is buried at Kensal Green Cemetery.

Abbreviations

A.	*An Autobiography*, ed. David Skilton (Harmondsworth: Penguin Classics, 1988)
BT	*Barchester Towers*, ed. John Sutherland (World's Classics; Oxford: Oxford University Press, 1996)
CYFH	*Can You Forgive Her?*, ed. Andrew Swarbrick (World's Classics; 2 vols. bound as one; Oxford: Oxford University Press, 1982)
DC	*The Duke's Children*, ed. Hermione Lee (World's Classics; 2 vols. bound as one; Oxford: Oxford University Press, 1982)
ED	*The Eustace Diamonds*, ed. W. J. McCormack (World's Classics; 2 vols. bound as one; Oxford: Oxford University Press, 1983)
FL	*Four Lectures*, ed. Morris L. Parrish (London: Constable, 1935)
FP	*Framley Parsonage*, ed. P. D. Edwards (World's Classics; Oxford: Oxford University Press, 1980)
HKWR	*He Knew He Was Right*, ed. John Sutherland (World's Classics; Oxford: Oxford University Press, 1985)
IHP	*Is He Popenjoy?*, ed. John Sutherland (World's Classics; 2 vols. bound as one; Oxford: Oxford University Press, 1986)
LCB	*The Last Chronicle of Barset*, ed. Stephen Gill (World's Classics; Oxford: Oxford University Press, 1980)
L.	*The Letters of Anthony Trollope*, ed. N. John Hall (2 vols.; Stanford, Cal.: Stanford University Press, 1983)
MF	*Marion Fay*, ed. Geoffrey Harvey (World's Classics; Oxford: Oxford University Press, 1992)
MM	*Miss Mackenzie*, ed. A. O. J. Cockshut (World's Classics;

Oxford: Oxford University Press, 1988)

NA *North America* (2 vols.; London: Chapman & Hall, 1862)

OF *Orley Farm*, ed. David Skilton (World's Classics; 2 vols. bound as one; Oxford: Oxford University Press, 1985)

PF *Phineas Finn*, ed. Jacques Berthoud (World's Classics; 2 vols. bound as one; Oxford: Oxford University Press, 1982)

PM *The Prime Minister*, ed. Jennifer Uglow (World's Classics; 2 vols. bound as one; Oxford: Oxford University Press, 1983)

PR *Phineas Redux*, ed. John C. Whale (World's Classics; 2 vols. bound as one; Oxford: Oxford University Press, 1983)

RH *Ralph the Heir*, ed. John Sutherland (World's Classics; 2 vols. bound as one; Oxford: Oxford University Press, 1990)

RR *Rachel Ray*, ed. P. D. Edwards (World's Classics; Oxford: Oxford University Press, 1988)

SHA *The Small House at Allington*, ed. James R. Kincaid (World's Classics; Oxford: Oxford University Press, 1980)

TC *The Three Clerks*, ed. Graham Handley (World's Classics; Oxford: Oxford University Press, 1989)

Th. *Thackeray* (London: Macmillan, 1879).

VB *The Vicar of Bullhampton*, ed. David Skilton (World's Classics; Oxford: Oxford University Press, 1988)

W. *The Warden*, ed. David Skilton (World's Classics; Oxford: Oxford University Press, 1980)

WWLN *The Way We Live Now*, ed. John Sutherland (World's Classics; 2 vols. bound as one; Oxford: Oxford University Press, 1988)

1

The Life and *An Autobiography*

Trollope opens his often elusive and provocative *An Autobiography* (1883) with an insistence that he will dwell on the facts of his public life rather than offer an analysis of the minutiae of his private life:

> In writing these pages, which, for the want of a better name, I shall be fain to call the autobiography of so insignificant a person as myself, it will not be so much my intention to speak of the details of my private life, as of what I... have done in literature, of my failures and successes, such as they have been, and their causes, and of the opening which a literary career offers to men and women for the earning of their bread. (*A.* 7)

This study will follow Trollope's direction in placing its primary emphasis on his writings, on his literary career, and on his stature as a writer rather than on his life. In Trollope's case, however, when and how he lived *do* bear significantly on what and how he wrote. His *Autobiography* is, for example, vital not just because it has an important place amongst his writings but also because it helps his readers to understand his writings. It opens up avenues of exploration which can lead his readers in often unexpected, sometimes frustrating, sometimes singularly fruitful, directions.

The very fact that Trollope chose to call this autobiography *An Autobiography*, with an indefinite article, is indicative of the ways in which he can disconcert us as readers. This is not *the* way in which he seeks to present himself to us, but simply *a* way of so doing. It stands beside his novels, his essays, his travel writings, and his other public statements not as an explanation or justification of them but as a supplement to them. It also gives them a specific context which is both biographical and historical. There is, of course, false modesty in the opening self-deprecation that this is 'the autobiography of so insignificant a person as myself', but this very statement of insignificance leads us on to the more troublingly significant assertion of the second paragraph:

> My boyhood was I think as unhappy as that of a young gentleman could well be, my misfortunes arising from a mixture of poverty and gentle standing on the part of my father, and from an utter want on my part of that juvenile manhood which enables some boys to hold up their heads even among the distresses which such a position is sure to produce. *(A. 7)*

What Trollope seems to be doing here is deliberately to measure himself against, and then distance himself from, the life and career of a fellow novelist: Charles Dickens. Trollope began his *Autobiography* in October 1875, some five years after Dickens's death and four years after the appearance of the first volume of John Forster's *Life of Charles Dickens* (December 1871). In this first volume Forster had quoted a fragment of Dickens's own (aborted) autobiography and had made public for the first time the 'secret agony' of the traumatic period in Dickens's boyhood when he had been obliged to work as a drudge in Warren's Blacking Warehouse, when his bankrupt father had been confined to the Marshalsea Prison and when his mother had appeared to be complicit in his suffering. Dickens's continuing shame, vulnerability, and sense of rejection had, Forster suggested, determined the tenor of much of what Dickens subsequently wrote. When Trollope read Forster's volume in February 1872, he wrote to George Eliot describing how 'distasteful' he had found the experience. He was particularly offended by the vulgar self-indulgence of both Dickens and his biographer.

> Dickens was no hero; he was a powerful, clever, humorous, and, in many respects, wise man; – very ignorant, and thick-skinned, who had taught himself to be his own God, and to believe himself to be a sufficient God for all who came near him; – not a hero at all. Forster tells of him things which should disgrace him, – as the picture he drew of his own father, & the hard words he intended to have published of his own mother; but Forster himself is too coarse-grained ... to know what is and what is not disgraceful; what is or is not heroic. (*L.* ii. 557–8)

When he came to the account of his own boyhood Trollope was determined not to be vulgar. He was also determined, it seems, to pull rank. When he calls himself 'a young gentleman' and refers to his father's 'gentle standing', he was distinguishing himself and his family not only from what he suspected was Dickens's and Forsters's 'coarse-grained' vulgarity but also from the root of their vulgarity – their ungentlemanly birth.

The idea of gentility and the problem of defining who was and who was not a gentleman preoccupied many Victorians. Both may seem something of an anomaly to most twentieth- and twenty-first century readers, but in order to understand much that is essential in the social fabric described in the fiction of the past modern readers need to recapture the import of now redundant definitions, distinctions, and prejudices. As Chapter 3 will argue, the problems of determining gentility and of defining the codes of gentlemanly behaviour in Trollope's novels are far from exclusively matters of snobbery. Much more so than in the Georgian and Regency periods, the upper and upper-middle classes of Victorian Britain felt themselves threatened by the manifest changes brought about by industrialism and urbanization. Middle-class men and women were now far more inclined to define themselves according to their achievement or their professional status than they were by blood and birth. To these issues I will return. Let it be simply said here that, despite the vagaries of his parents and the financial insecurities of his own childhood, Trollope seems to have felt secure about his own gentlemanly status. Moreover, when his narrators and his predominantly 'genteel' characters discuss class (which they readily do), they discuss it aware of a threat to the old order of things presented by those whom they suspect to be 'coarse-grained' parvenus, intruders, and outsiders.

Trollope, who was born in April 1815, was descended on his father's side from a line of Lincolnshire baronets.[1] His grandfather, the fifth son of the fourth baronet, was a Cambridge graduate who after ordination served as the rector of two Hertfordshire parishes. His father, Thomas Anthony Trollope, educated at Winchester and Oxford, had determined on a legal career, was called to the bar in 1804, and practised in the Court of Chancery. This is the traditional kind of rooted, upper-middle-class, professional background which will be shared by many of Trollope's most stalwart characters. His mother, Frances Milton, the daughter of a Winchester- and Oxford-educated Hampshire parson, was, however, the granddaughter of a tradesman, albeit a prosperous Bristol saddler. We may, therefore, read a certain edge into the assertion made by Mrs Freeborn, the doctor's wife in *The Two Heroines of Plumpington* (1882), that it 'always does take three generations to make a gentleman'. There is certainly an implied criticism of Sir Peregrine Orme's narrow definition of rank in *Orley Farm* (1861–2): 'A gentleman, according to his ideas, should at any rate have great-grandfathers capable of being traced in the world's history; and the greater the number of such, and the more easily traceable they might be on the world's surface, the more unquestionable would be the status of the claimant in question' (*OF* i. 28).

Despite such ripples of snobbish dissent, Trollope clearly believed that his gentlemanly pedigree mattered. What disturbed him in boyhood was his parents' inability to maintain the proper dignity of their social standing. His father's legal career, which had never prospered, was wrecked by his moodiness and irascibility. The steady failure of a crucial investment in property at Harrow was to accentuate a sense of having been slighted by the world and having had his life wrecked by forces beyond his control. Even Thomas Anthony Trollope's ambitious attempt at scholarship, an *Encyclopaedia Ecclesiastica*, only got as far as a single volume covering the letters A (for 'Abaddon') to F (for 'Funeral Rites'). Trollope was doubtless thinking of his father's psychological problems when he remarked in his novel set in the family's Harrow property, *Orley Farm*: 'There is nothing perhaps so generally consoling to a man as a well-established grievance; a feeling of having been injured, on which his mind can brood from hour to hour, allowing him to plead his own cause in his own court, within his own heart – and always to plead it successfully' (*OF* i. 81). His father's solitary gloom may also have contributed to his portraits of the obsessional Louis Trevelyan in one of his very finest novels, *He Knew He Was Right* (1868–9), and of the disappointed lawyer, Sir Thomas Underwood, in *Ralph the Heir* (1870–1). By contrast, his mother's active, and to modern readers singularly valiant, attempts at restoring the family's broken fortunes seem to have struck her son as ill-advised and embarrassing. In 1827 Frances Trollope left her moody husband in Harrow and set sail for America, where she established an exotic commercial bazaar in Cincinnati, Ohio, which combined art galleries, a concert hall, and a coffee house with an attempt to sell imported knick-knacks to frontiersmen. Her enterprising, and certainly bizarre, investment (which came to be known as 'Trollope's Folly') proved a failure, but her extended American sojourn had one profitable outcome: her sharp and unflattering study, *Domestic Manners of the Americans*, of 1832. Although the book raised many American hackles, it created a favourable stir in Britain and helped to establish Frances Trollope's subsequently flourishing literary career. She was to go on to write some thirty-five novels. With two such 'literary' parents it is scarcely surprising that three of the surviving Trollope siblings should later have turned to fiction (Anthony was to produce forty-seven novels; his elder brother, Thomas Adolphus, twenty; his younger sister, Cecilia, who died young, but one). In *An Autobiography* Trollope is temperate both in his posthumous praise of his mother's creative energy and in his compensatory criticism of it and her:

> Book followed book immediately... She refurnished the house which I have called Orley Farm, and surrounded us again with moderate comforts. Of the mixture of joviality and industry which formed her character it is impossible to speak with exaggeration... She was at her table at four in the morning and had finished her work before the world had begun to be aroused. But the joviality was all for others... Her power of dividing herself into two parts, and keeping her intellect by itself, clear from the troubles of the world and fit for the duty it had to do, I never saw equalled. I do not think that the writing of a novel is the most difficult task which a man may be called upon to do; but it is a task that may be supposed to demand a spirit fairly at ease... She was endowed too much with creative power, with considerable humour, and a genuine feeling for romance. But she was neither clear sighted nor accurate; and in her attempts to describe morals, manners, and even facts, was unable to avoid the pitfalls of exaggeration. (*A.* 21, 24, 27)

This is an awkward tribute from one writer to another. Trollope acknowledges his mother's dedication and sheer hard work (something he was to imitate in his own literary career), and he is self-deprecating about the art of novel-writing (his own as much as her's), but he seems to be ill as ease with her achievement (both as a mother and as a role model). He was to be far less kind about the hack novelist, and the indulgently dysfunctional parent, Lady Carbery, in *The Way We Live Now* (1874–5). The picture of Lady Carbery has long been taken to be an oblique glance back at Frances Trollope:

> She did work hard at what she wrote, – hard enough at any rate to cover her pages quickly; and was, by nature, a clever woman. She could write after a glib, commonplace, sprightly fashion, and had already acquired the knack of spreading all she knew very thin, so that it might cover a vast surface. She had no ambition to write a good book, but was painfully anxious to write a book the critics should say was very good... The woman was false from head to foot... (*WWLN* i. 17)

Lady Carbery is determined to succeed and she uses all the wily charm that she can muster to influence her male publishers and critics in her favour. We can assume that Frances Trollope did likewise. Despite her reputation as a writer, the ageing, but still pushy, Mrs Trollope does not seem to have universally impressed those who met her. In the 1850s the schoolboy Sabine Baring-Gould found her a 'good-humoured, clever, somewhat vulgar old lady' while Robert Browning warned his wife against 'that coarse, vulgar Mrs Trollope... that vulgar pushing woman.'[2] In his fastidious, 'gentlemanly', and masculine way Trollope himself may well have felt embarrassed not simply by what his mother had written, but also by the manner in which she, like the equally ambitious and penurious Lady Carbery, had attempted to promote herself and her writings in a male-dominated society.[3]

If Trollope felt that Dickens's criticisms of the hurts and embarrassments caused by his parents were 'coarse-grainedly' direct, his own adverse comments on his immediate family are by comparison oblique. As *An Autobiography* makes clear, however, he felt the 'misfortunes arising from a mixture of poverty and gentle standing' acutely. This was particularly true of his somewhat wayward educational career. Trollope's elder brothers, Thomas Adolphus and Henry, had been sent as day boarders to Harrow School, and here at the age of 8 in 1823 Anthony joined them. Harrow was still basking in the afterglow of the raffish Lord Byron's time at the school, but the Trollope boys, on charity scholarships for village boys, were largely excluded from the aristocratic, or at the very least genteel, companionship which Anthony craved. During his three years at Harrow he remained the despised junior boy of the school and endured a 'daily purgatory' in running from his home to a school at which most boys boarded. There then followed a period at a private school in Sunbury and then, at the age of 12, he again followed his brothers to his father's old school, Winchester College. What may, in other boys' cases, have marked the beginning of new friendships and the opening of a privileged future was for Trollope a miserable extension of his former educational purgatory. His elder brother, Thomas Adolphus, persecuted him and, as a result of his family's financial embarrassments, his college bills and his pocket money went unpaid. 'My schoolfellows of course knew it was so', he later commented, 'and I became a Pariah' (*A*. 12). Not only was he ill-dressed and dirty; he felt that he was 'big, and awkward, and ugly' (*A*. 12). He also experienced an acute period of loneliness. His father's desultory career having collapsed and his fortunes having further deteriorated, Trollope was removed from Winchester and sent back to Harrow again as a day boy. These eighteen months, when he lived alone with his brooding and preoccupied father, he later regarded as 'the worst period of my life... I was now over fifteen, and had come to an age in which I could appreciate at its full the misery of expulsion from all social intercourse' (*A*. 13). There was also no prospect of his being sent to a university. Nevertheless, Trollope's years at public school left him with a good grasp of Classics and a particular taste for Latin literature (notably the poetry of Horace), which is evident in his citations of favourite authors in his novels. In 1870 he was to publish a translation of *The Commentaries of Caesar* (he considered Julius Caesar 'the greatest name in history') and ten years later he finished what he called the 'magnum opus for my old age', *The Life of Cicero*.

When he was 19, the Trollope family's fortunes took another turn for the worse: their property was seized by bailiffs and in the spring of 1834 they were obliged to decamp to Belgium in order to live more cheaply than they could in England. In their Bruges lodgings, nursed by his mother, Trollope's brother Henry died of consumption; his sister Emily fell victim to the same mortal disease, and his increasingly frail father attempted to work away at his ecclesiastical encyclopaedia (he too was to die in Belgium in October 1835). Trollope was reduced to feeling that he was 'an idle, desolate hanger on, that most hopeless of human beings, a hobbledehoy of nineteen without any idea of a career, a profession, or a trade' (*A*. 23).

The months in Belgium marked the lowest ebb in the family's fortunes. In November 1834, however, the 'hobbledehoy' was to enter the profession which was to transform his sense of his own worth and potential. Having escaped the prospect of an alternative career as an officer in the Austrian cavalry, he was nominated to a clerkship in the General Post Office in St Martins-le-Grand in London. This appointment was thanks to a connection of his mother's, Mrs Clayton Freeling, the wife of the Secretary of the Stamp Office, who had in turn prevailed upon her father-in-law, Sir Francis Freeling, the Secretary of the Post Office from 1797–1836. The Post Office was then virtually a private fiefdom of the Freeling family and appointments such as Trollope's were in Sir Francis's gift. The system ran by means of a complex pattern of family connection, patronage, graft, nods, and winks. As such it was not unlike other branches of the civil service, nor, in effect, did it differ much from the satirical picture of the Circumlocution Office presented by Dickens in *Little Dorrit* (a picture which Trollope found distasteful). The civil service was not to be reformed, by the introduction of competitive examinations, until the 1850s. Trollope himself was merely examined by another son of Sir Francis, Henry, who asked him to copy out some lines from *The Times* (which he blotted) and questioned him about his proficiency in mathematics (he was vague in his reply). After being told that he would be re-examined on the following day, he in fact found that no further hurdles were placed in his path. Surprising as it may seem to modern readers, Trollope was to remain consistent in his opposition to competitive entry to the civil service, firmly believing as he did in the gentlemanly propriety of the system by which he had been recruited. As he insisted in *An Autobiography*:

> There are places in life which can hardly be well filled except by 'gentlemen'... It may be that the son of the butcher in the village shall become as well fitted for employments requiring gentle culture

> as the son of the parson. Such is often the case. When such is the case no one has been more prone to give the butcher's son all the welcome he has merited than I myself; – but the chances are greatly in favour of the parson's son. The gates of the one class should be open to the other; – but neither to one class nor to the other can good be done by declaring that there are no gates, no barrier, no difference. The system of competitive examination is I think based on a supposition that there is no difference. (*A.* 31)

As his novels also make clear, for Trollope good breeding was evident not only in how a gentleman acted, but also in what could be expected of him.

Trollope's years a junior clerk in the office of the Secretary of the GPO were, by his own account, years of drudgery in which he 'very soon achieved a character for irregularity' (he claimed that he had a watch that was always ten minutes late). When Sir Francis Freeling was succeeded as Secretary by Colonel Maberly in 1836 he found himself working for a man who was 'certainly not my friend' (*A.* 34). During his time working under Maberly he was treated, he said, as though he were unfit for any useful work and felt that he was always on the point of being dismissed despite his 'striving to show how good a public servant I could become, if only a chance were given me' (*A.* 35). Much of the office drudgery and the compensating private diversions that Trollope experienced during this period later found their way into the account he offered of civil-service life in his novel *The Three Clerks* (1858) (though the Post Office is here translated into the purely fictional 'Office of the Board of Commissioners for Regulating Weights and Measures', generally supposed to be 'a well-conducted public office'). In *Marion Fay* (1881–2), which *does* touch on the duties of gentlemanly clerks in the GPO, Colonel Maberly appears in the guise of the officious Sir Boreas Bodkin, known to his underlings as 'Aeolus'. Trollope's memories of bachelor life in a London boarding house also inform the experience of the worthy John Eames, a clerk in the Income Tax Office, described in *The Small House at Allington* (1862–4).

In July 1841 Trollope's professional career took a decisive turn for the better when he applied to Maberly for one of the newly created posts of clerks to the regional Postal Surveyors (there were seven Surveyors for England, two for Scotland, and three for Ireland). Clerks travelled over the districts assigned to the Surveyors reporting at regular intervals on accounts and on the deficiencies in the postal arrangements under their supervision. Despite the general conviction amongst the clerks at St Martins-le-Grand that 'nothing could be worse than the berth of a Surveyor's clerk in Ireland', Trollope was appointed to replace the clerk for the Irish Central District, who had apparently proved 'absurdly incapable' in his post (Trollope had been lucky enough to be the first person in the GPO to read the report of this incompetence when it arrived in London). When Maberly appointed him to Ireland, Trollope firmly believed that the secretary was heartily glad to be rid of him. He arrived in Banagher, King's County (now Co. Offaly), after a long journey by canal boat from Dublin on 19 September. From here he travelled widely on official business through the province of Connaught. His journeys were gradually to extend into all four provinces of Ireland and were to give him an intimate, if privileged, knowledge of Irish life. In August 1844 he was transferred to Clonmel, Co. Tipperary, to work under the Surveyor for the Southern District. Here, having at long last discovered a taste for hard, responsible, and deliberate work, he proved assiduous in his attention to his duties, exposing lax service and corrupt and readily corruptible local postmasters. He was also able to observe at first hand the relative poverty of Ireland and, from 1845, the devastating effects of the Potato Famine. Although he particularly relished the company of the Irish gentry, and tended to interpret the problems and grievances of Ireland from the paternalistic perspective of its landowners, his five Irish novels (*The Macdermots of Ballycloran* (1847), *The Kellys and the O'Kellys* (1848), *Castle Richmond* (1860), *An Eye for an Eye* (1878–9), and *The Land-Leaguers* (1882–3)) suggest that he was at ease in the Irish countryside and that he had established an acute and sympathetic engagement with a broad cross-section of Irish rural life. In Ireland, and with Irish material, he began his career as a writer of fiction. He was to use this material more extensively and consistently than any other English novelist of the nineteenth century.

In Ireland, too, Trollope discovered his lifelong passion for hunting. As he noted in *An Autobiography*:

> I have ever since been constant to the sport, having learned to love it with an affection which I cannot myself fathom or understand...it has been for more than thirty years a duty to me to ride to hounds, and I have performed that duty with a persistent energy. Nothing has ever been allowed to stand in the way of hunting, – neither the writing of books, nor the work of the Post Office, nor other pleasures. (*A.* 45)

To many readers' dismay, hunting scenes appear at regular, and sometimes distracting, intervals throughout his fiction (the first such is in *The Kellys and the O'Kellys*); a crucial twist in the plot of *Ralph the Heir* is occasioned by an untimely death in a hunting accident; Francis Tregear's injuries sustained in a similar accident in *The Duke's Children* (1879–80) help change the Duke's attitude to him; the eight *Hunting Sketches* of 1865 describe, with an insider's knowledge, the commitment of eight riders to hounds, and *The Land-Leaguers* devotes no fewer than three chapters to fox-hunting in Galway. Nevertheless, what Trollope appears to have most appreciated about the hunting field in Ireland was its easy bonhomie and sense of classless comradeship. As we now know, he was also to affirm his belief in classless, male comradeship by becoming a freemason in Ireland. His Irish years served not only to cement his new-found self-confidence and professional dedication; they also provided, through the medium of fox-hunting, a model of cooperative, relaxed, relatively tolerant, hospitable, gentlemanly society in which chance was countered with skill, intelligence was married to play, and danger was matched by bravado. In a strange way some of these sporting qualities were to manifest themselves in Trollope's often floundering third novel, *La Vendée: An Historical Romance* (1850), a highly charged fiction centred on the Royalist insurrection in western France of the 1790s, a counter-revolutionary movement which allied the aristocracy, the gentry, and a conservative peasantry.

In the summer of 1842 Trollope met Rose Heseltine, his future wife, while she was on holiday with her family at Kingstown (now Dun Laoghaire), then a middle-class watering place close to Dublin. He makes no mention of his two-year courtship of Rose in *An Autobiography* and is somewhat curt in his references both to his marriage in June 1844 and to his new wife's family: 'My marriage was like the marriage of other people and of no interest to any one except my wife and me. It took place at Rotherham in Yorkshire, where her father was manager of a bank' (*A.* 50). He was not being discourteous to Rose, for his marriage was to prove, as far as we can tell, an extremely happy one, but he was perhaps exercizing a gentlemanly tact in regard to her origins and to a skeleton in her family cupboard. Rose's father was what Trollope would have taken for a provincial tradesman, a man who had risen to the position of the manager of the Rotherham office of the Sheffield and Rotherham Joint Stock Company. He had flirted with Unitarianism, was a director of the Sheffield and Rotherham Railway, and privately indulged what we might presume to be a romantic side to his character by collecting armour. It may well have proved an expensive hobby. In 1854, after his retirement to Torquay, he was discovered to have tampered with the bank's books to the extent of some £4,000 or £5,000. He fled to France in order to escape prosecution and died there, a broken man, in 1855. It is probably mistaken to speculate about the degree to which Edward Heseltine's crime may have inspired those of Trollope's financially corrupt fictional villains (ungentlemanly upstarts such as Ferdinand Lopez or Augustus Melmotte). What is certain, however, is that after their marriage the Trollopes had singularly little to do with the surviving members of the Heseltine family.

In August 1851, thanks to his reputation for the successful reorganization of rural deliveries in the south of Ireland, Trollope was appointed to a temporary post in the South-Western division of England in order to supervise the extension there of rural postal services (this was a particular concern of the energetic new Secretary to the Postmaster General, the celebrated Sir Rowland Hill). From his base in Exeter, Trollope was, over a period of two years, to travel extensively through the western and south-western counties of England. His brief also included the Channel Islands. He had been familiar with the cathedral city of Exeter since his boyhood (the city was to figure prominently in both *Rachel Ray* (1863) and *He Knew He Was Right*) but it was during a professional visit to Wiltshire in May 1852 that Barchester, its cathedral and its close, first implanted itself in his imagination. He describes the incident in *An Autobiography*:

In the course of this job I visited Salisbury and whilst wandering

> there on a midsummer evening round the purlieus of the Cathedral I conceived the story of *The Warden*, – from whence came that series of novels of which Barchester with its bishops, deans, and archdeacon was the central site. I may as well declare at once that no one at the commencement could have had less reason than myself to presume himself able to write about clergymen… I never lived in any Cathedral city, – except London, never knew anything of any Close, and at that time had enjoyed no peculiar intimacy with any clergyman. (*A.* 63)

Trollope is being disingenuous both about his knowledge of clergymen and clergy manners and about his experience of cathedral cities (in addition to his knowledge of Exeter he had lived in Winchester as a schoolboy and during his inspection of the Hereford post office he had also visited a cousin in the 'sweet close'). It is true, however, that Barchester, and its surrounding county of Barset, seem to float rather than be anchored in a specific geographical locality. His fourth novel, *The Warden* (1855), opens with an insistence on this non-specificity ('Were we to name Wells or Salisbury, Exeter, Hereford, or Gloucester, it might be presumed that something personal was intended'). Barchester and Barset are clearly in the south and west of England, and, as readers begin to get further acquainted with the social and physical geography of the county in the later Barsetshire novels (*Barchester Towers* (1857), *Doctor Thorne* (1858), *Framley Parsonage* (1860–1), *The Small House at Allington* (1862–4), and *The Last Chronicle of Barset* (1866–7)), it becomes evident that Trollope has amalgamated aspects of Devon, Somerset, and Wiltshire in shaping his imaginary shire. These novels were to prove his most steady and lasting successes with his growing reading public.

It was in the course of his professional visit to St Helier in Jersey in November 1851 that Trollope put forward the case for the introduction of roadside letter boxes, iron 'pillar boxes', such as were already in use in neighbouring France. What was wanted, he explained to his superiors in London, was 'a safe receptacle for letters, which shall be cleared on the morning of the despatch of the London mails'. His idea was approved by the Postmaster General and the first boxes were erected in St Helier in November 1852. Such was the success of the experiment that it was extended to Guernsey in February, to England in

September, and to Ireland in March 1855. Trollope was modestly proud of having been the 'originator' of the letter box, and of the service that he had introduced. In *He Knew He Was Right* he nevertheless wryly allowed one of his more outrageously conservative characters, the redoubtable Miss Jemima Stanbury, who lives in the close at Exeter, considered objections to the innovation:

> As for the iron pillar boxes which had been erected of late years for the receipt of letters, one of which, – a most hateful thing to her, – stood almost close to her own hall door, she had not the faintest belief that any letter put into one of them would ever reach its destination. She could not understand why people should not walk with their letters to the respectable post-office instead of chucking them into an iron stump, – as she called it, – out in the middle of the street with nobody to look after it. (*HKWR* 69)

But then, as Trollope himself recognized, the inhabitants of cathedral closes, whether clerical or lay, were not necessarily sympathetic to innovation, however publicly beneficial.

After the completion of his two-year secondment to England, Trollope, his wife and his two sons (Henry b. 1846 and Frederic b. 1847), returned to Ireland. He was now acting surveyor of the Northern District, his formal appointment to the post being made in October 1854. In January 1858 he was commissioned by 'the great men at the General Post Office' to go to Egypt in order to arrange a postal treaty which would facilitate the movement of mails to and from India. On this trip he was also to inspect postal operations at Malta and Gibraltar and to visit Jerusalem. This was the first of several significant official overseas visits (he was sent out to 'cleanse the Augean stables' of the West Indian Post Office in the following November, visiting Cuba and Puerto Rico in the process). It was also to mark the beginning of a series of extended foreign trips, both official and private, which were to render Trollope the best travelled of all Victorian writers. His extensive, busy, and sometimes fraught roamings beyond Europe were not only to be reflected in the exotic settings of certain of his novels, (notably *The Bertrams* of 1859) they were also to form the basis of four of his travel books: *The West Indies and the Spanish Main* (1859), *North America* (1862), *Australia and New Zealand* (1873), and *South Africa* (1878).

In the summer of 1859 Trollope finally left Ireland for the post of Surveyor of the Eastern District of England (which included the three East Anglian counties as well as Huntingdonshire and the eastern parts of Hertfordshire and Bedfordshire). The Trollopes set up home at Waltham Cross in Essex, in easy reach of both London and the counties in his charge. He was also able to hunt regularly. His twelve years at Waltham Cross were to be singularly productive both in terms of his official duties and, more significantly, in terms of his burgeoning literary output. As he proudly noted of his extraordinary, and perhaps typically Victorian, energy in *An Autobiography*:

> I feel confident that in amount no other writer contributed so much during that time to English literature. Over and above my novels I wrote political articles, critical, social, and sporting articles for periodicals without number. I did the work of a Surveyor of the General Post Office, and so did it as to give the authorities of the department no slightest pretext for fault-finding. I hunted always at least twice a week... Few men I think ever lived a fuller life, and I attribute the power of doing this altogether to the virtue of early hours. It was my practice to be at my table every morning at 5.30 a.m., and it was also my practice to allow myself no mercy. (*A.* 174)

During his years with the GPO Trollope had learned the virtues of time-keeping and organization. He wrote systematically, some might say almost mechanically, in three-hour stretches, with his watch in front of him, setting himself the target of producing 250 words every quarter of an hour. His habit of rising early to write, and his rigid self-discipline, may also have helped to give his narratives their particularly lucid quality, their clarity, straightforwardness, and their sharpness of purpose. His prose style is certainly plain and unexperimental. When he complains in *An Autobiography* of the idiosyncrasies in Dickens's style (which he sees as 'jerky, ungrammatical, and created by himself in defiance of rules' (*A.* 160)), Trollope may indeed be suggesting that his own readers should particularly take pleasure in the stylistic conformity and consistency of his English prose.

Trollope's last seven years in the service of the GPO were to be notable for the ten substantial novels that he found time to write during them. These include *Framley Parsonage, Orley Farm, The Small House at Allington, Can You Forgive Her?* (1864–5), and *The Last Chronicle of Barset*. These were the novels which were to mark the apogee of his popularity and esteem with the Victorian reading public. This was also the period of his association with the most significant new journal of the 1860s, the superbly illustrated *Cornhill Magazine*. At its inception in January 1860 the *Cornhill* was edited by the contemporary writer whom Trollope most admired, Thackeray. The admiration was mutual, for Thackeray was later to tell him that *The Three Clerks* was the only novel that, in his experience, had kept him awake after dinner. The *Cornhill*'s publisher, George Smith, wanted to serialize 'an English tale, with a clerical flavour' (*A*. 94). Trollope accordingly went to work 'on these orders' and presented Smith with the completed first half of a new 'Barsetshire' novel, *Framley Parsonage*, within two months of signing the agreement. He had in fact written the first forty-eight pages of manuscript in the first five days. Much of the success of the first monthly issues of the *Cornhill* (it sold 110,000 copies) was indeed due to the popularity of Trollope's new novel. It was given pride of place in the magazine, while Thackeray's own story, *Lovel the Widower*, was relegated to later pages. The serialization of *Framley Parsonage* was also to be marked by the beginning of a singularly fruitful partnership between the novelist and his finest illustrator, the painter John Everett Millais. Millais was later to provide fine sets of illustrations for *The Small House at Allington* (also serialized in the *Cornhill*) and for *Orley Farm*, which the novelist considered to be 'the best I have seen in any novel in any language' (*A*. 110).

The literary success that Trollope enjoyed in the 1860s was to lead to his departure from the GPO in October 1867. Although he had always failed to establish a satisfactory working relationship with his superiors, and notably with Sir Rowland Hill, Trollope had been happy in his choice of profession. His main incentive for abandoning his career was financial. When he was offered the editorship of the new journal, *Saint Pauls Magazine*, with a salary of £750, he found himself independent and free to pursue his growing political ambitions (the magazine was to be a vehicle for his distinctive variety of independent Liberalism). In the first number of the journal he declared that 'of all studies to which men and women can attach themselves . . . the first and foremost' was politics. *Saint Pauls* was to contain two of his best political novels, *Phineas Finn* (serialized

1867–9 with illustrations by Millais) and *Ralph the Heir*. As Chapter 4 will argue, Trollope the novelist was a particularly astute observer of the political process and of the pressures exerted on and by politicians. Like many upright and otherwise intelligent people before and since his time, he was not to prove a very adept politician himself. In *Can You Forgive Her?* (1864–5) he had written of the entrance to the House of Commons:

> It is the only gate before which I have ever stood filled with envy, – sorrowing to think that my steps might never pass under it . . . I have told myself, in anger and in grief, that to die and not to have won that right of way, though but for a session . . . is to die and not to have done that which it most becomes an Englishman to have achieved . . . It is the highest and most legitimate pride of an Englishman to have the letters M.P. written after his name. (*CYFH* ii. 44)

In the summer of 1868 Trollope agreed to stand in the Liberal interest for the borough of Beverley in the East Riding of Yorkshire. Beverley had a reputation for electoral skulduggery and he himself described it on the eve of his departure for the election campaign as 'one of the most degraded boroughs in England.' Trollope's own account of the unpropitious opening of his campaign in *An Autobiography* is nicely wry, despite the evident bitterness which underlies it:

> the gentleman who acted as my agent . . . understood Yorkshire . . . He understood all the mysteries of canvassing, and he knew well the traditions, the condition, and the prospects of the liberal party . . . 'So,' said he, 'you are going to stand for Beverley!' I replied gravely that I was thinking of doing so. 'You don't expect to get in!' he said. Again I was grave. I would not, I said, be sanguine, but nevertheless I was disposed to hope the best. 'Oh no,' continued he, with good humoured raillery, 'you won't get in. I don't suppose you really expect it. But there is a fine career open to you. You will spend £1000, and lose the election. Then you will petition and spend another £1000. You will throw out the elected members, there will be a commission, and the borough will be disfranchised. For a beginner such as you are that will be a great success.' (*A*. 191)

His agent's 'understanding' proved to be accurate enough. Trollope spent 'the most wretched fortnight of his manhood' in canvassing. He was no public speaker, his statements of his political principles were greeted with indifference, and his opponents employed a combination of outright bribery, graft, and manipulation which he could neither afford nor believed in. He spent £400, was rejected by the voters, and, after an official inquiry into its electoral corruption, the borough was duly disfranchised. He summed his experience up succinctly: 'Beverley's privilege as a borough, and my parliamentary ambition, were brought to an end at the same time' (*A*. 194). The débâcle at Beverley was, however, to leave one enduring legacy. In April 1869, some five months after his defeat, Trollope began work on *Ralph the Heir*. The novel contains an acidly comic account of an election at 'Percycross' (the Percy family were closely linked to Beverley in the fifteenth century). The 'Percycross' candidate, the morose and lazy lawyer Sir Thomas Underwood, may not bear a close resemblance to the novelist himself, but Sir Thomas's disillusionment with the processes of Victorian electioneering certainly echoes Trollope's own.

In October 1860, during a visit to his brother Tom's villa in Florence, Trollope had met a 21-year-old American woman, Mary Katherine Keemle Field (commonly known as 'Kate'). He was to establish his intimate friendship with Kate Field in the United States in both 1861 and 1868 and during her extended periods of residence in England in the 1870s; he was also to correspond with her both regularly and affectionately. Her impact on Trollope is evident in the tribute he pays to her in Chapter 17 of *An Autobiography*. After speaking generally about American characteristics he launches suddenly into a fulsome digression:

> There is an American woman, of whom not to speak in a work purporting to be a memoir of my own life, would be to omit all allusion to one of the chief pleasures which has graced my later years. In the last fifteen years [he was writing in 1876] she has been, out of my family, my most chosen friend. She is a ray of light to me from which I can always strike a spark by thinking of her... I could not write truly of myself without saying that such a friend had been vouchsafed me. I trust that she may live to read the words I have now written, and to wipe away a tear as she thinks of my feeling while I write them. (*A*. 201)

The relationship was clearly sexually charged on Trollope's part, but it was almost certainly unconsummated in the physical sense. His wife, Rose, seems to have tolerated both its existence and her husband's infatuation. What appears to have attracted him to this younger woman was her vivacity, vibrancy, intelligence, and independence of mind, qualities which were to mould many of his best-observed women characters in the novels of the 1860s and 1870s. She may not have been the precise model on which a Glencora Palliser, a Lucy Robarts, or a Lily Dale is based, and she was surely no Lizzie Eustace, but she was certainly, like the sharp and patient Rose Trollope, the kind of woman that Trollope recognized as both a soulmate and an equal. The fact that Trollope was to dedicate an entire chapter of his *North America* to a discussion on 'The Rights of Women' probably reflects something Kate's determined feminism and his own equally determined 'chivalric' arguments against her ('The best right a woman has is the right to a husband . . .' (*NA* i. 408)). She was, in a platonic sense, his other love, his other half, and his other wife. When he wrote of the recently deceased Thackeray in February 1864 that 'One loved him almost as one loves a woman, tenderly and with thoughtfulness, – thinking of him when away from him as a source of joy which cannot be analysed, but is full of comfort,'[4] it was doubtless also of Kate that he was thinking.

In May 1871 the Trollopes sailed from Liverpool to Melbourne, ostensibly to visit their younger son, Fred, who had emigrated to Australia in 1865. Trollope worked steadily on a new novel, *Lady Anna*, during the voyage, averaging nine pages a day and missing only one day through illness. They were to spend a year touring Australia before visiting New Zealand and returning to Britain via the United States (where Trollope briefly and inconsequentially met the Mormon leader, Brigham Young, in Salt Lake City). After their nineteen-month absence they took a respectable upper-middle-class house in Montagu Square in London, where they were to remain until 1880. Here he built up a good working library of some 5,000 volumes, a collection rich in drama (particularly of the seventeenth century) and Latin literature. At Montagu Square in May 1873 Trollope began his most scathing commentary on the multiple corruptions of modern life, *The Way We Live Now*. The satire in this, his thirty-second novel, 'went beyond the iniquities of the great speculator who robs everybody, and made an onslaught also on other vices, – on the intrigues of girls who want to get married, on the luxury of young men who prefer to remain single, and on the puffing propensities of authors who desire to cheat the public into buying their volumes' (*A.* 225). Despite its stress on 'modern' life, *The Way We Live Now* also owes a distinct debt to Trollope's reading, both to the representation of a morally shifty London in the work of Jonson, Middleton, and Massinger and to the attacks on the corruptions of Imperial Rome in the work of Martial, Cicero, and Horace (indeed it has been suggested that the very title of the novel derives from Cicero[5]). Perhaps because of their satirical edge, neither *The Way We Live Now* nor its successor, *The Prime Minister* (1875–6), was to achieve the popular success of the novels of the 1860s.

Trollope made a return visit to Australia in 1875, continuing work on a new novel, *Is He Popenjoy?* (1877–8) on the voyage out. He completed it the day before he arrived in Melbourne and then went on to work on *The American Senator* (published 1876–7). He returned to England via New Zealand, Hawaii, San Francisco ('I do not know that in all my travels I ever visited a city less interesting to the normal tourist' (*A.* 221)), Boston and New York. During the sea-trip home he attracted the discriminating attention of a fellow passenger, the young Henry James. James, who was later to write one of the best appreciations of Trollope's 'genius', was evidently not personally taken with the novelist, 'who wrote novels in his state room all the morning... and played cards... all the evening. He has a gross and repulsive face and manner, but appears *bon enfant* when you talk with him. But he is the dullest Briton of them all.'[6] Trollope was not in fact writing 'novels' during the voyage (he had finished *The American Senator* on American soil), but working on his *Autobiography,* which he was to complete in April 1876. In many ways *An Autobiography* is an assessment of what Trollope believed that he had achieved as a writer, in both quality and quantity. He was proud to have outwritten his contemporaries and claimed that, 'if any English authors not living have written more' (*A.* 230), he did not know who they were. His literary productivity remains phenomenal by any standards and his consistent quality and range effectively unequalled. *An Autobiography* was also a summing-up of his life to date and offers something of a personal valediction. He always intended that it should be published posthumously, but through its final pages runs a virtually unspoken acknowledgement that his best years, both as a writer and as a man, were now over.

Trollope had at least two more major works in him, his critical/biographical study of Thackeray and his fine novel about the slow dissolution of a dissolute and unscrupulous old man, *Mr Scarborough's Family* (published posthumously 1882–3). In the late 1870s and early 1880s he was to continue travelling, though now only within Europe, but he gave up hunting, after thirty-five years of riding to hounds, in the spring of 1876. In July 1880, finding London noisy and distracting, he and his wife 'retired' to the village of South Harting on the borders of Sussex and Hampshire. Here he continued writing (including a book on the late Prime Minister, Palmerston, and his novel about new twists in the 'Irish problem', *The Land-Leaguers*). He was constitutionally incapable of vegetating, but age, illness, and bouts of boredom took their toll. During a visit to London in November 1882 he suffered a stroke which paralysed his right side. He was virtually incapable of speech during his last weeks and died on 5 December. He was buried at Kensal Green Cemetery three days later, not far from the grave of Thackeray. *An Autobiography* was published in October 1883.

2

Trollope the Critic and his Contemporaries

Anthony Trollope, born in 1815, the year of Waterloo, was one of an extraordinary generation of English novelists, a generation perhaps unequalled in variety, scope, and talent in British literary history. It was a generation that came to maturity in the first decades of Queen Victoria's reign and its work continues to shape how successors have come to view 'Victorian' literature. It included Elizabeth Gaskell, born 1810; William Makepeace Thackeray, born 1811; Charles Dickens, born 1812; Charlotte Brontë, born 1816; Emily Brontë, born 1818, George Eliot, born 1819 and Anne Brontë, born 1820. It was a generation which grew up under the benign shadow of the works of Sir Walter Scott and under the heady influence of Romanticism (both British and European). Had not the term 'Victorian' established itself long ago, it was a generation which might well be known in literary-historical terms as 'post-Romantic'.

Trollope was well aware of the literary tradition in which he found himself and of the work of those contemporaries against whom he measured himself and his art. He also had ambitions as a literary critic and a literary historian. Early on in his career he had contemplated writing a vast 'History of World Literature' (though the 'World' defined here would probably have been a singularly Eurocentric one). In the 1860s he resumed an aspect of this unwieldy project by preparing notes for a 'History of English Prose Fiction', a history which would have begun with Sidney's *Arcadia* and ended with Scott's *Ivanhoe.* Had the project been realized it would doubtless have been highly, and to some modern eyes, intrusively opinionated (he had, for example, found Aphra Behn's novels 'detestable trash'), but it would also have attempted, daringly enough, 'to describe how it had come to pass that the English novels of the present day have become what they are, to point out the effects which they have produced, and to enquire whether their great popularity has on the whole done good or evil to the people who read them' (*A.* 139). Here, as throughout his comments on fiction, Trollope tends to look on literary criticism as part moral exercise and part a 'vindication' of his own professional status as a 'realist' writer. His criticism of the tradition in which he worked was, as it was in the instances of S. T. Coleridge, Matthew Arnold, and T. S. Eliot, essentially a means of reflecting on the nature of his own contribution to the tradition (or what we might call the 'canon'). His favourite novelists were to remain Sir Walter Scott, Thackeray, and, to a lesser degree, Jane Austen. As he explained in the third chapter of *An Autobiography,* these predilections were formed early in his career. Writing of his adolescent reading he noted: 'I had already made up my mind that *Pride and Prejudice* was the best novel in the English language, – a palm which I partially withdrew after a second reading of *Ivanhoe* and did not completely bestow elsewhere till *Esmond* was written [in 1852]' (*A.* 32). When he lectured in 1870 on 'English Prose Fiction as a Rational Amusement', it was on these three authors that he again placed his major emphases (*FL* 94–124, 128, 133–4). In this lecture he argued that Scott's novels had 'inaugurated altogether a new era in Prose Fiction' and insisted that since Scott's time the British had 'become a novel reading people' and that 'all our other reading put together hardly amounts to what we read in novels' (*FL* 97). From Scott, he argued, there stemmed a new seriousness, not only in terms of how a novelist conceived of his or her work, but also in terms of how readers received and appreciated the fiction presented to them.

In many ways Trollope's defined taste for the work of Austen, Scott, and Thackeray suggests useful ways of defining both his own art as a novelist and his approach to novel-writing. This was evidently as true in his own day as it is in ours. An anonymous, and generous, reviewer of Trollope's first novel, *The Macdermots of Ballycloran,* in 1847 had claimed to find in it a 'dramatic power akin to that we find in Sir Walter Scott's novels'.[1] At the time of his death at least two Victorian critics drew parallels between his novels and those of Austen. One, writing in *The Times,* somewhat patronizingly suggested that neither was a writer of the first rank, but that both stood 'at the head of the second order'; the other, writing in the *Spectator*, saw both primarily as social commentators and their novels as a means of assessing the changes that had taken place 'between the rural life of Miss Austen's pictures and the rural life of Mr Trollope's'.[2] As to the pre-eminence of Thackeray's influence, we shall return to it later in this chapter. What needs to be stressed here is that both his first critics, and indeed Trollope himself, saw him as a realist, and recognized that his 'inestimable merit' lay in what Henry James acutely called his 'complete appreciation of the usual'.[3] It is through Trollope's criticism of other writers, and through his own comments on his work, that we can best determine the distinctive nature of that realism.

On a superficial level, as we have seen, Trollope's prejudices against Dickens and his work were based on a suspicion of Dickens's vanity and self-assertiveness. Dickens represented the outward face of the vulgarity that Trollope most distrusted, both as man and as an author. Dickens was also famously, and unmistakably, caricatured in Chapter 15 of *The Warden* as 'Mr Popular Sentiment', a novelist, propagandist, and would-be reformer who overstates the case against Mr Harding by misperceiving it in a novel called *The Almshouse*. Trollope's narrator lets the veil of fiction slip when he goes on to damn with high praise:

> Mr Sentiment's great attraction is in his second-rate characters. If his heroes and heroines walk upon stilts...their attendant satellites are as natural as though one met them in the street...yes, live, and will live till the names of their calling shall be forgotten in their own, and Buckett and Mrs Gamp will be the only words left to us to signify a detective police officer or a monthly nurse. (*W.* 206)

Dickens, Trollope readily acknowledges elsewhere, has real power as a writer, but it is a sporadic power, more likely to make itself felt in his representations of eccentricity than in his pictures of everyday respectability and probity. He argues in his 1870 lecture on English Prose Fiction, for example, that Dickens's ordinary characters 'have not the likeness to human nature' (*FL* 129) which he so readily found in Thackeray. For Trollope the problem with Dickens lay partly in his failure as a true 'realist' and, more substantially, in the nature of his vast popularity with contemporary readers:

> The primary object of a novelist is to please; and this man's novels have been found more pleasant than those of any other writer. It might of course be objected to this that though the books have pleased, they have been injurious; – that their tendency has been immoral and their teaching vicious; – but it is almost needless to say that no such charge has ever been made against Dickens... From all which there arises to the critic a question whether, with such evidence against him as to the excellence of this writer, he should not subordinate his own opinion to the collected opinion of the world of readers. (*A.* 159)

Despite the force of received opinion, he places Dickens's work in a lower category than that of Thackeray and George Eliot. But then, as he had reason to know, mere popularity does not make for a secure critical base. In the generally laudatory obituary of Dickens that he wrote for *Saint Pauls Magazine* in 1870, Trollope referred, somewhat snobbishly, to Dickens's skill in tapping into 'the ever newly-growing mass of readers as it sprang up among the lower classes'.[4] There may, of course, be a tinge of professional jealousy in his repeated references to Dickens's vast sales, but Trollope's criticism seems to be rooted in a suspicion that his rival was more of an exploiter of his readers' emotions than he was a flatterer and refiner of them. Dickens emerges throughout Trollope's criticism of him as a writer who wore his heart too much on his sleeve, one who manipulated his readers by a combination of a 'drollery' and a pathos which was ultimately 'stagey and melodramatic' (*A.* 159). Trollope does not define what he means by the 'stagey and melodramatic', but we can suppose that, in common with George Eliot in her essay on the German realists,[5] he is happy to disparage Dickens's departures from what he assumes are the proper norms of realism. This 'theatrical' bent seems to have offended Trollope in more ways than the purely 'literary'. In a letter of 1875 he tetchily compared Dickens's 'self-consciousness and irritated craving for applause' with that of the actor W. C. Macready (*L.* ii. 671). Dickens was 'stagey' by instinct, an aspect of his life and art which was clear enough to his contemporaries both in his self-projection as a reader of his own works and in the manner in which he shaped the dialogue in his eminently 'actable' fictions. Ironically, it is precisely Dickens's departures from, distortions of, and experiments with commonly accepted nineteenth-century 'realist' norms of representation which have most attracted those latter-day critics who have seen nineteenth-century realism as something of a straitjacket from which so much subsequent literature needed to free itself.[6]

Trollope felt far more comfortable with George Eliot, both as a fellow realist and as a friend. The two writers met in 1860, when Trollope impressed Eliot with what she called his 'straightforward, wholesome *Wesen* [personality]'. Within two years she was flatteringly referring to him as 'our excellent friend . . . one of the heartiest, most genuine, moral and generous men we know'.[7] When she read *Orley Farm* in 1862 she wrote to a friend to express her deep appreciation of the novel, asserting that 'Trollope is admirable in the presentation of even, average life and character, and he so thoroughly wholesome-minded that one delights in seeing his books lie about to be read'.[8] Having become a determined reader of his novels, she was later to admit to a fellow novelist that she was 'not at all sure that, but for Anthony Trollope, I should ever have planned my studies on so extensive a scale for *Middlemarch*, or that I should, through all its episodes, have persevered with it to the close'.[9] In *An Autobiography* Trollope proclaimed her 'at the present moment [1876] . . . the first of English novelists', though second to deceased Thackeray in his personal canon. He was, however, troubled by Eliot's intellectuality:

> the nature of her intellect is very far removed indeed from that which is common to the tellers of stories. Her imagination is no doubt strong, but it acts in analysing rather than creating. Everything that comes before her is pulled to pieces so that the inside of it shall be seen, and be seen if possible by her readers as clearly as by herself . . . In her, as yet, there is no symptom whatever of that weariness of mind . . . It is not from decadence that we do not have another Mrs Poyser, but because the author soars to things which seem to her to be higher than Mrs Poyser . . . It is I think the defect of George Eliot that she struggles too hard to do work that shall be excellent. (*A.* 157–8)

It is not surprising, therefore, that Trollope should have retained the conviction that *Adam Bede* was her best novel and have doubted in *An Autobiography* whether 'any young person can read with pleasure either *Felix Holt, Middlemarch,* or *Daniel Deronda*' (*A.* 157–8). Although he wrote glowingly in June 1862 to congratulate her on the first number of the serialization of her historical novel *Romola* in the *Cornhill Magazine,* he had none the less warned her as a fellow professional that she tended 'to fire too much over the heads' of her readers and added: 'You have to write to tens of thousands, & not to single thousands' (*L.* i. 186–7). When he had praised *Felix Holt* to her in August 1866, he suggested that the novel's 'great glory' was 'the fullness of thought which has been bestowed on it' (*L.* i. 346). He does not appear to have ventured to criticize *Daniel Deronda* to her face, but he told another correspondent in 1876 that he had found it 'trying' and 'all wrong in art' because of its author's 'striving for effects which she does not produce' (*L.* ii. 789).

What Trollope most appreciated about Eliot's work was precisely what she found most admirable about his own, the quality of the representation of 'even, average life and character'. Although it is an easy enough exercise to recognize parallels between Trollope's and Eliot's studies of clerical and provincial life, it is essentially in their shared and vivid sensitivity to the details of ordinary human intercourse that they are most closely related as novelists.[10] Trollope clearly did not respond very happily to the increasingly cerebral and epic developments in Eliot's fiction in the late 1860s and 1870s. In an important way he saw his own work as forming a middle way between Dickens's exaggerated pandering to the masses and the narrower, and potentially alienating, intellectual ambitions of Eliot's later novels. In avoiding abstraction as rigorously as he eschewed sensationalism, he was happily prepared to accept the quotidian limitations of what he insisted was the hallmark of modern realism.

Although he does not refer directly to Eliot in 'On English Prose Fiction as a Rational Amusement', the influence of her early work pervades Trollope's assessment of the desiderata of good, moral, realist fiction. He does, however, introduce brief and telling reference to the novels of both Charlotte Brontë and Elizabeth Gaskell. He was not personally acquainted with either writer and he probably did not know of Gaskell's delighted remark of March 1860 to their shared publisher, George Smith, expressing the wish that 'Mr Trollope would go on writing

Framley Parsonage for ever'.[11] When he notes of Gaskell's novels that they are 'quite worthy of being mentioned as works of art that have done their good by their teaching while they have charmed by their grace and truth' (*FL* 121), he may sound merely plodding – unless, that is, we accept that he is acknowledging a profound literary sympathy with her achievement. His praise of Charlotte Brontë is ostensibly equally bland:

> she also possessed a power of minutely seeing and describing the inner work of the heart which belonged so remarkably to Thackeray... Circumstances had hidden from her much of the outside world, she was feeble in health, and prone, as all who are isolated, to be too conscious of her own self. This consciousness she displays in her writing to a fault; but her power and honesty of purpose, and intention to do good... are not to be doubted. (*FL* 122)

This looks like a flat enough recitation of the Brontë 'myth' unless we pause at the mention of Thackeray (which would certainly have flattered Brontë herself) and at the stress laid on her observation of nature. As *An Autobiography* makes plain, what particularly delighted Trollope about *Jane Eyre* was what he saw as its successful balance of the 'realistic' and the 'sensational':

> The readers who prefer the one are supposed to take delight in the elucidation of character. Those who hold by the other are charmed by the construction and gradual development of a plot. All this is I think a mistake, – which mistake arises from the inability of the imperfect artist to be at the same time realistic and sensational. A good novel should be both, – and both in the highest degree. (*A.* 146)

His references to *Jane Eyre* in this section of *An Autobiography,* in the same context as *Ivanhoe, Henry Esmond,* and his own *Orley Farm,* suggest the true degree of his appreciation of Brontë's achievement.

As we have seen, Trollope returns repeatedly both in his criticism and in his own fiction to the example of Thackeray. Thackeray is the first novelist referred to in Chapter 13 of *An Autobiography* ('On English Novelists of the Present Day'). He is declared to be paramount because his characters 'stand out as human beings with a force and truth which has not... been within the reach of any other English novelist in any period.' (*A.* 156). Trollope singles out the characterization of Colonel

Newcome in *The Newcomes* (1853–5) for special praise:

> It is not because Colonel Newcome is a perfect gentleman that we think Thackeray's work to have been so excellent, but because he has had the power to describe him as such and to force us to love him, a weak and silly old man, on account of this grace of character. (*A.* 156)

Trollope was, of course, drawn instinctively to Newcome simply because of his gentlemanliness, but he also recognizes the fact that readers were not presented with an *ideal.* Thackeray emerges as the supreme realist, as the witty and generous truth-teller. In 'English Prose Fiction as a Rational Amusement' the point is emphasized:

> Thackeray with his minute feminine glances into life, seeing the workings of the human heart with that magnifying glass with which nature had supplied him, could not paint his portraits in the Raphaelistic manner. He saw what there was of good and evil in men and women, and he had to put it all down. (*FL* 119)

Thackeray is therefore a subtle and suggestive artist not a facile and idealizing one. He paints observantly, but unflatteringly. As such he created a Lady Castlewood (in *Henry Esmond*) 'a woman all over, – generous, self-devoting, full of jealousy, angry without cause, unjust, irrational, full of faith, full of piety, and true as steel' than whom Trollope thought 'nothing finer can be found in the whole range of English Prose Fiction' (*FL* 120).

This witty, subtle, protean Thackeray also emerges in Trollope's own novels, both as a point of reference and as a standard by which readers are bidden to assess the art of his disciple. Trollope's references can be merely whimsical (such as the naming of a Thackerayan footman in *Barchester Towers* 'James Fitzplush', or a borrowing of the pseudo-aristocratic name 'Cinquebars' in *Can You Forgive Her?*). They can also be more nuanced and substantive. In the last chapter of *The Small House at Allington* (serialized in the *Cornhill Magazine* under Thackeray's editorship), Lily Dale jokes that 'you mustn't believe a word of what that bad man says in his novels about mothers-in-law' (*SHA* 665) (a reference to Thackeray's general hostility to the species), and in Chapter 92 of *He Knew He Was Right* the narrator refers to the 'great master' who alerted his contemporaries to the multi-layered significance of English snobbery.

Again, towards the end of *Ralph the Heir* Trollope's narrator adopts a distinctly Thackerayan tone when he apologizes for having described the adventures of a man who was not 'fit to be delineated as a hero' (*RH* i. 337). But then, as he goes on to point out, 'for one Henry Esmond, there are fifty Ralph Newtons' (*RH* i. 338). The precedent of Thackeray's 'minute feminine glances into life' was certainly a factor in shaping the boldness and intelligence of certain of his own women characters. The provocative shade of Becky Sharp haunts *The Eustace Diamonds* (1871–3). As with Becky we are told that Lizzie Eustace cannot be dignified with the status of a 'heroine' and Lizzie effectively proves herself a Becky *rediviva* both in her unscrupulousness and in her uncanny success as a performer (like her 'she always made use of her child when troubles came'). Readers are also likely to recognize the Thackerayan nuances of the statement in Chapter 17 that Lizzie 'was made to sparkle' and was a woman who 'ought to wear diamonds'. The narrator then adds the crucial proviso: 'The only doubt might be whether paste diamonds might not better suit her character' (*ED* i. 159).

Trollope's most extended tribute to Thackeray's art is the critical biography of his hero that he contributed to the English Men of Letters Series in 1879. Although the book lays repeated and unflattering stress on Thackeray's habitual indolence ('unsteadfast, idle, changeable of purpose . . . no man ever failed more generally than he to put his best foot foremost' (*Th.* 19), it probably does so because mention of such casualness serves to heighten Trollope's personal belief in the redemptive powers of dedication and hard work.[12] In a memorable passage later in his study, one ostensibly praising the composition of *Henry Esmond*, Trollope seems in fact to be describing his own methods of work:

> The author can sit down with the pen in his hand for a given time, and produce a certain number of words. That is comparatively easy, and if he have a conscience in regard to his task, work will be done regularly. But to think it over as you lie in bed, or walk about, or sit cosily over your fire, to turn all in your thoughts, and make things fit, – that requires elbow-grease of the mind. (*Th.* 123)

Thackeray, it is implied, lacked drive, not mental 'elbow-grease', genius, or originality. The wonder of the narrative invention of *Vanity Fair* is duly pressed on readers by means of a contrast with two of Dickens's early novels and their respective heroes:

> Thackeray, who never depended much on his plot in the shorter tales which he had hitherto told, determined to adopt the same form [as the monthly-part issue of *Pickwick Papers* and *Nicholas Nickleby*] in his first great work, but with these changes; – That as the central character with Dickens had always been made beautiful with unnatural virtue, – for who was ever so unselfish as Pickwick, so manly and modest as Nicholas, or so good a boy as Oliver? – so should his centre of interest be in every respect abnormally bad. (*Th.* 26)

In conceiving of a 'novel without a hero' in *Vanity Fair,* Thackeray had radically shifted the focus of the received models of English fiction, decisively moving away from the ideal to the real. Not only had he moved a Becky Sharp and her 'abnormal badness' to centre stage; he had also played an 'unheroic' William Dobbin against her. 'Dobbins exist', Trollope insists, 'and therefore Thackeray chose to write of a Dobbin' (*Th.* 94). Nevertheless, Dobbin, in common with Henry Esmond and Colonel Newcome, can properly exhibit a 'true nobility' because he is presented as an instinctive, generous-spirited, if largely passive, gentleman.

Trollope's unfaltering admiration for *Esmond* above all other Thackeray novels informs his study from beginning to end. *Esmond* might ostensibly seem to be the novel that least influenced his own fiction. It is a historical novel, but Trollope's floundering *La Vendée* bears no real resemblance to it. It is a first-person narrative, but that is a form that he generally eschewed. It is a novel marked by what Thackeray called 'cut-throat melancholy', scarcely a notable characteristic of any of Trollope's significant works. What certainly attracted Trollope was its principal women characters, Rachel and Beatrix, but neither has an obvious Trollopian progeny. A key to the influence of *Esmond* may lie in its being at the core of Thackeray's loosely realized plan of linking his novels together through ancestral and family structures so that the Esmonds, the Warringtons, the Crawleys, and the Pendennises would all prove to be connected by blood.[13] But then, Trollope's own use of connections, characters, and places between novel and novel is contemporary rather than ancestral. Where *Esmond* matters as a reference point within Trollope's work is that it provided a model to be aspired to rather than imitated. It certainly touched him personally. Its often elusive, self-pitying, and disconcerting first-person narrative tone may in fact have influenced *An Autobiography* far more than it shaped any of Trollope's pure fictions.

Trollope's novels seem far closer in spirit to *Vanity Fair*, *Pendennis*, and *The Newcomes*. It is in these novels that Thackeray's sharply ironic presentation and playful narrative manipulation of his characters combine with a witty deftness of expression and a seemingly incongruous, but none the less determining, geniality. The three novels also seem distinctly less 'weighty' in their moralizing than does the mature, didactically insistent, fiction of George Eliot. Thackeray's comedy can be shot through with an awareness of a pervasive moral corruption, with pain or death or what we might loosely term 'tragedy', but they never topple over into the purely tragic, whether personal or social. Indeed, tragedy, in its classical form, seems to have struck both Thackeray and Trollope as too dangerously akin to the 'heroic' and the 'ideal' and therefore alien to the essence of modern, essentially middle-class 'realism'. Trollope learnt his lesson as a moralist from the example of Thackeray, but he also received it as a novelist content to work in a long and worthy comic tradition. It was to this tradition that George Meredith addressed himself in his *Essay on Comedy and the Uses of the Comic Spirit* in 1877. Although he mentions neither Thackeray nor Trollope by name, like them Meredith sees English bourgeois respectability as resistant to what he calls 'the Comic Spirit' because English respectability finds comedy disconcerting:

> They [a large middling body of opinion 'neither Puritan nor Bacchanalian'] have a sentimental objection to face the study of the actual world. They take up disdain of it, when its truths appear humiliating: when the facts are not immediately forced on them, they take up the pride of incredulity. They live in a hazy atmosphere that they suppose an ideal one. Humourous writing they will endure, perhaps approve, if it mingles with pathos to shake and elevate the feelings. They approve of Satire, because, like the beak of the vulture, it smells of carrion, which they are not. But of Comedy they have a shivering dread, for Comedy enfolds them with the wretched host of the world, huddles them with us all in an ignoble assimilation, and cannot be used by any exalted variety as a scourge and a broom.[14]

It is probably significant that neither Meredith nor Thackeray nor Trollope has yet been satisfactorily 'placed' in an agreed, or even readily received canon, of English fiction. Each was in his own way an uneasy 'Victorian', and yet all three have, unlike Dickens or the Brontës or George Eliot, or even Henry James, steadily failed to find themselves established in exalted places in a post-Victorian critical pantheon. If we seek for a justification for this relative neglect, it may well be a direct, and perhaps surprising, consequence of the fact that Trollope's comic adjustments of strict 'realism', like those of Thackeray and Meredith, continue to have a power to disconcert.

As a critic himself Trollope has none of Meredith's provocative edge or analytical nicety. When, for example, he speaks of his own leading principles as a novelist, he is often as bland in his expression as he is lax in his definitions. In 'English Prose Fiction as a Rational Amusement' he defines what he means by a novel with a narrow insistence on the importance of amatory interest.

> The book which we call a novel contains, we may say, always a love story. Indeed, taking the general character of novels as our guide, we may say that the love stories are their mainstay and the staff of their existence. They not only contain love stories, but they are written for the sake of the love stories. They have other attractions, and deal with every phase of life; but other attractions hang around and depend on the love story as the planets depend upon the sun. There are novel worlds, no doubt, in which the planets are brighter than the sun; in which the love-making is less interesting than the life by which it is surrounded, but these are erratic worlds, novels out of the course of nature, and to be spoken of as exceptional. (*FL* 108–9)

Where does this leave *Robinson Crusoe* or *Tristram Shandy* or *Pickwick Papers* or *Oliver Twist* one is tempted to ask? What Trollope is defining, of course, is his own norm of a novel to the exclusion of other norms and other variants. The notion of the centrality, or rather the necessity, or some kind of love story is related not only to his appreciation of the work of Thackeray and Eliot but also to his sense of the importance of modern realism. He is describing not the redundant heroics of ancient epics or medieval romances, but the concerns and preoccupations of ordinary middle-class men and women who, without being remotely elevated, fall messily in and out of love. Nor is he concerned with the egotistical individualism of the Romantics, but with social virtues, with communality, and with personal relationships (whether working, grating, or fracturing). In Chapter 12 of *An Autobiography* he reiterates the point by insisting that 'very much of a novelist's work must appertain to the intercourse between young men and young women.' If *Pickwick* be accepted as an exception to the rule, he suggests, even in that novel 'there are three or four sets of lovers whose little amatory longings give a softness to the work.' Even when he attempted to write a novel without romantic interest, as he says he began to do in *Miss Mackenzie*, he still felt himself obliged 'to make her [his heroine] fall in love at last' (*A.* 144).

When Trollope insists in the same chapter that he is essentially 'realistic' as a writer, he is distinguishing himself from the writers of what was called at the time 'sensation' fiction (notably Wilkie Collins and M. E. Braddon). Again his stress is on the representation of ordinary human experience rather than of the extraordinary:

> No doubt a string of horrible incidents bound together without truth in details and told as affecting personages without character, – wooden blocks who cannot make themselves known to the reader as men and women, – does not instruct or amuse or even fill the mind with awe. Horrors heaped upon horrors, and which are horrors only in themselves and not as touching any recognised and known person, are not tragic and soon cease even to horrify. (*A.* 146)

Trollope seems here to be associating 'sensation fiction' with the by now musty Gothic mode of the early part of the century. He was not averse, of course, to introducing murder, mayhem, and mystery into his own fiction (think, for example, of *Phineas Redux* (1873–4) or *The Vicar of Bullhampton* (1869–70) or *He Knew He Was Right* or the novel Trollope himself mentions in this context, *Orley Farm*), but he seeks to condition sensationalism with the commonplace much as he subsumes tragedy in a basically benign and comic narrative framework. These principles he sums up yet again in an insistence on veracity and truth-to-life: 'Truth let there be; – truth of description, truth of character, human truth as to men and women. If there be such truth I do not know that a novel can be too sensational' (*A* 147). Trollope attempts to be consistent in terms both of his representation of character and of the society that has moulded character. He also sees consistency as vital to the very shaping of his narratives. This is evident in what he says of his use of dialogue, though here he allows for a series of provisos:

> [a novelist] is not allowed, for the sake of his tale, to make his characters give utterance to long speeches such as are not customarily heard from men and women. The ordinary talk of ordinary people is carried on in short sharp excessive sentences which very frequently are never completed, – the language of which even among educated people is often incorrect. The novel-writer in constructing his dialogue must so steer between absolute accuracy of language, – which would give to his conversation an air of pedantry, – and the slovenly inaccuracy of ordinary talkers, – which if closely followed would offend by an appearance of grimace, – as to produce upon the ear of his reader a sense of reality. (*A.* 154)

He is well aware that a writer of fiction shapes his or her characters' speech patterns as much as he or she determines how, where, and why characters act or fail to act. Trollope's 'realism' is, as he acknowledges, merely an attempt at truthful representation, an attempt which remains bounded by established conventions of fictionality. Just as by conditioning the effects of 'sensation' he creates an impression of the ordinary, so, he trusts, his narrative consistency gives an air of probability.

Something of the determining quality of Trollope's 'realism' has been discussed by some of his best twentieth-century critics.[15] It is perhaps indicative of the relative neglect of Thackeray's fiction, however, that there does not seem to have been a parallel spate of modern critical interest in *his* once vaunted 'realism'. Thackeray's critics seem most often content to categorize him in equally loose terms as a 'satirist' (the word that Meredith warns us to be careful with). What should alert Trollope's readers to the ancient, and also solidly Thackerayan, comic tradition in which he stands is his use of suggestive names for places and for his minor characters. These names can playfully and punningly vary from the seat of the Dukes of Omnium, Gatherum Castle ('omnium gatherum' was a common Victorian pseudo-latinism for a gathering of things and people) and the name of Archdeacon Grantley's living, Plumstead Episcopi (it is a plum living in the gift of the bishop), to a Barchester Doctor called Fillgrave, a London breeches-maker called Neefit, a German feminist called Baroness Banmann, and a firm of lawyers called Slow and Bideawhile. This is not the kind of nomenclature that we would expect in a novel by Austen or Eliot, but these are names that could well have been met with in a seventeenth-century play, an eighteenth-century comic novel, or indeed a twentieth-century satirical magazine such as *Private Eye*. Trollope will play in the tradition of give-away naming, but at the same time he will determinedly avoid creating (or re-creating) character-types such as Jonson or Fielding would have happily employed. But that is precisely where Thackeray's presence in an alternative 'great tradition', a predominantly comic, moral, and satiric tradition, is so crucial to our understanding of the nature, variety, and status of Trollope's work.

Unlike Dickens, Trollope cannot properly be seen as a proto-Modernist or as a writer who had to wait for due critical recognition in a more susceptible twentieth century. He saw himself as a post-Romantic 'realist' who acknowledged parallels between his work and that of Eliot and Gaskell, but he is not a realist in the sense that Zola is, nor can he be related to the kind of 'gritty' realism favoured by twentieth-century documentary film-makers. He was a realist working in the long moral comic tradition which links Fielding's, Smollett's, and Thackeray's novels to those of the Dickens that he both distrusted and disliked. Put another way, like Meredith, he acknowledged that the comic tradition which he had adapted to suit his own narrative prejudices and predilections was disconcerting because it sought to see two sides to an argument, and the two sides of a given character or situation, simultaneously but, unlike Fielding or Smollett or Dickens, non-judgementally. He explains this, with a sharpness often absent from his more obviously detached essays in literary criticism, to the readers of Chapter 18 of one of the most vital and challenging of his novels, *The Eustace Diamonds*:

> Within the figure and frame and clothes and cuticle, within the bones and flesh of many of us, there is but one person, – a man or woman, with a preponderance either of good or evil, whose conduct in any emergency may be predicted with some assurance of accuracy by any one knowing the man or woman. Such persons are simple, single, and perhaps, generally, safe. They walk along lines in accordance with certain fixed instincts or principles, and are to-day as they were yesterday, and will be to-morrow as they are to-day... But there are human beings who, though of necessity single in body, are dual in character; – in whose breasts not only is evil

> always fighting against good, – but to whom evil is sometimes horribly, hideously evil, but is sometimes also not hideous at all... Such men, – or women, – may hardly, perhaps, debase themselves with the more vulgar vices. They will not be rogues, or thieves, or drunkards, – or, perhaps, liars; but ambition, luxury, self-indulgence, pride and covetousness will get hold of them, and in various moods will be to them virtues in lieu of vices. (*ED* i. 163–4)

Here is Trollope the Thackerayan moralist. As he acknowledges, a Lizzie Eustace and a Lucy Morris can both be, in their opposite ways, *consistent* in their choices between vice and virtue, while a Frank Greystock appears as ambiguous without necessarily being morally categorized as vicious or virtuous. In Chapter 35 of the same novel Trollope's narrator addresses his reader in an equally Thackerayan vein on a related aspect of their shared narrative art:

> the reading world [has] taught itself to like best the characters of all but divine men and women. Let the man who paints with pen and ink give the gaslight, and the flesh-pots, the passions and pains, the prurient prudence and the rouge-pots and pounce-boxes of the world as it is, and he will be told that no one can care a straw for his creations. With whom are we to sympathise? says the reader, who not unnaturally imagines that a hero should be heroic. Oh, thou, my reader, whose sympathies are in truth the great and only aim of my work, when you have called the dearest of your friends round you to your hospitable table, how many heroes are there sitting at the board?... Our own friends around us are not always merry and wise, nor, alas! always honest and true. They are often cross and foolish, and sometimes treacherous and false. They are so, and we are angry. Then we forgive them, not without a consciousness of imperfection on our own part. And we know – or, at least, believe, – that though they be sometimes treacherous and false, there is a balance of good. We cannot have heroes to dine with us. There are none. (*ED* i. 318–19)

Trollope's narrator speaks directly to his readers, not with a tone of Olympian detachment or of moral censure, but as an intimate, tolerant, and worldly-wise companion. Nineteenth-century novels cannot properly have heroes, he implies, because heroism is no longer a familiar or comfortable virtue and because the epic is no longer a viable literary form. Heroism can be neither socialised or domesticated. This is the essential lesson that Trollope learnt from Thackeray's fiction and this is why, despite critical resistance to the idea, he chose to call himself a realist.

3

Trollope and Class

Benjamin Disraeli's most lasting legacy to the rhetoric of British politics is the phrase 'the two nations'. It served originally as the subtitle to his novel *Sybil* (1845) and readers were alerted to its significance in a now famous dialogue between the aristocratic hero, Egremont, and the Chartist agitator, Morley:

> 'Well society may be in its infancy,' said Egremont slightly smiling; 'but, say what you will, our Queen reigns over the greatest nation that ever existed.'
>
> 'Which nation?' asked the younger stranger, 'for she reigns over two.'
>
> The stranger paused; Egremont was silent but looked inquiringly.
>
> 'Yes,' resumed the younger stranger after a moment's interval. 'Two nations between whom there is no intercourse and no sympathy; who are as ignorant of each other habits, thoughts and feelings, as if they were dwellers in different zones or inhabitants of different planets; who are formed by a different breeding, are fed by a different food, are ordered by different manners, and are not governed by the same laws.'
>
> 'You speak of –' said Egremont, hesitatingly.
>
> 'THE RICH AND THE POOR'.[1]

Disraeli's capital letters here clearly indicate that this is a debating point. Indeed, his novel as a whole is an attempt to open up the debate concerning what contemporaries called 'the condition of England question'. Thanks to the influence of Thomas Carlyle, the idea of the potential conflict between 'haves' and 'have-nots' was particularly current in early Victorian political and social discourses, concerned as those discourses were with the increasingly unsettling impact of industrialization and urbanization. The medieval division of the kingdom into three estates was no longer either readily acceptable or particularly feasible. Moreover, the idea of the representation of the three estates in Parliament, as the Houses of Lords and Commons, was increasingly questioned in the debates which attended the passage of the 1832 Reform Bill. Disraeli's bipartite division also effectively dispensed with the well-established assumption that there were upper, middle (or 'middling'), and lower classes (not yet uniformly referred to as 'working' class or classes). His redefinition of the nation as starkly divided into the rich and the poor, and therefore into those who owned property – and hence exercised power – and those who were propertyless and powerless, cut across the old estates and assumed that a substantial, generally mercantile, section of the old middle-class 'commons' had moved up into the 'ruling' class. Disraeli's division has, nevertheless, established itself not simply as political rhetoric but as a commonly held prejudice about the nature of Victorian society.

The prejudice was significantly reinforced by Marx and Engels, who, from a German perspective, had insisted in *The Communist Manifesto* of 1848 that European, and not merely British, society had fundamentally changed in the post-French Revolutionary era:

> The modern bourgeois society that has sprouted from the ruins of feudal society has not done away with class antagonisms. It has but established new classes, new conditions of oppression, new forms of struggle in place of the old ones.
>
> Our epoch, the epoch of the bourgeoisie, possesses, however, this distinctive feature: it has simplified the class antagonisms. Society as a whole is more and more splitting up into two great hostile camps, into two great classes directly facing each other. Bourgeoisie and Proletariat.[2]

The Marxist notion of two opposed classes in industrialized society, and of the historical dialectic of class struggle, has been profoundly and often distortingly influential. For Marx and Engels, revolutions in the nature of production, the opening of world markets, and the free exchange of capital, as opposed to the old dependence on agriculture and land ownership, had radically and irreversibly shifted the organization of modern society, effectively removing influence from the old aristocracy and empowering an aggressive and upwardly mobile, urban bourgeoisie. For Marx and Engels, the old, 'feudal' society had ceased to function politically.

This is no place to engage in the extended debate as to how, when, and why that radical change may have occurred. Society *had* changed fundamentally in the first half of the nineteenth century, but it had not necessarily changed in the way that Disraeli and Marx insisted that it had. Rather than being divided into two great, historically opposed classes, early- and mid-Victorian Britain in fact saw a redefinition of the middle class as much as it witnessed the formation of a new working class.[3] The redefinition of the middle class necessarily embraced a whole variety of divisions and subdivisions, from the old gentry and professional classes at the top to the respectable petty bourgeoisie and upper artisans (Marx's 'intermediate class') at the bottom. That Trollope, in common with many other novelists, both contemporary and subsequent, chose to write exclusively about the upper reaches of society should not necessarily suggest that he was cutting himself off from an urgent contemporary debate. What needs to be noted in any discussion of Trollope's fiction is that he was observing a flourishing society which seems to be only marginally concerned with radical social change. It could be argued that, because he established his reputation as a writer in the late 1850s and 1860s rather than in the far more troubled late 1830s and 1840s, he simply missed out on the fashion for 'condition of England fiction' that marked not only the literary careers of Disraeli, Kingsley, Gaskell, and Dickens but also that of his mother (the author of *Michael Armstrong, The Factory Boy* of 1839).[4] The urgency of that Carlyle-inspired fashion had certainly been dissipated by 1860, largely because the England of the 1850s had proved to be far more consolidated and stable, both socially and economically, than the England of the 1840s.[5] Trollope certainly gives his readers a narrowly focused view of nineteenth-century England, one which substantially excludes representations of working-class life, but it ought not to be inferred that he therefore gives us a distorted or peripheral view. Trollope's novels reflect a substantial, prosperous, assured, class-conscious, middle- and upper-class England, but not an England actively engaged in class struggle nor a neurotic nation fatally divided against itself. They offer us a representation of middle-class England redefining itself rather than ring-fencing itself. The redefinition is taking place not in the face of a threat from below, but as a consequence of a general expansion of economic opportunity and a related diminution of old barriers between classes.

Trollope's Britain functions with its industrial base kept at a safe and clinical distance. Trollope's Manchester is merely the city that the attorney's clerk, Fred Pickering, leaves in the short story, 'The Adventures of Fred Pickering' (1867), though he returns to a legal career there once his attempt to forge himself a new life in London fails. Trollope's Birmingham functions as the setting of the International Legal Conference that takes place in *Orley Farm*. Trollope's Leeds is where a rum group of 'commercial gentlemen' meet up in the Bull Inn in the same novel. Trollope's Sheffield, Wolverhampton, Preston, Sunderland, Glasgow, or Belfast seem not to exist at all. Trollope's England is either London-based or county-townish, agricultural, and traditional. It is most commonly peopled by gentlemen landowners, by shabby-genteel dowagers of both sexes, by lawyers, doctors, clergymen, and civil servants. As the only omnipresent representatives of the working classes, even his servants do their job silently. Trollope's Scotland is a land of lairds and lochs, not of smokestacks and shipyards. Trollope's Ireland is either rural, poor, and honest or rural, genteel, and on horseback. It would be absurd to say that Trollope's England, Scotland, and Ireland did not actually exist as he pictures them, but it is certainly true that until recently most modern observers chose not to look at the nineteenth-century United Kingdom in a Trollopian light. They declined to do so because historically grounded prejudices dictated alternative emphases on particular urban, or commercial, or proletarian, or nationalist dynamics. Readers of Victorian novels had come to anticipate dramatizations of social problems, gender distinctions, and political dilemmas rather than representations of provincial continuity, moral conservatism, and the surprising adaptability of 'middle England'. Trollope's novels are centrally concerned with an old England which had emphatically not disappeared in the nineteenth century. It is an England which prospers, as it had since the seventeenth century, by means of inherited money, advantageous marriage settlements, discreet investment, and the shrewd management of property, through the maintenance of professional status, professional codes, and professional fees. His England is often cumbrous and substantially unreformed, with a fudging legal system, a crusty and boorish aristocracy, an Erastian Church, and an unrepresentative Parliament. Trollope's favoured corner of southern England, Barsetshire, can be as constrictingly provincial as Flaubert's Normandy, and its parsonages and manor houses can seem to be as remote from a metropolitan mainstream as any estate in Turgenev's Russia, but it and its inhabitants function, thrive, and prosper none the less. But then even Barsetshire is no sleepy hangover from Jane Austen's England. It is linked by a burgeoning railway system to the main centres of economic power and political influence; its postal services run with due efficiency and expedition; the press, both local and national, render it attentive to what London says and what London does, and it knows the weight it carries in national and ecclesiastical affairs. Trollope's England may not ostensibly resemble that of Disraeli or Marx, or, for that matter, of Dickens, but to his many Victorian readers it was emphatically and recognizably a modern England.

Trollope's England, and the Scotland and Ireland that happily coexist on its margins, is an old society in the sense that it has remained substantially untouched by the industrial revolution and by the consequent 'class consciousness' that so exercised the political minds of Disraeli and Marx. It was not, of course, isolated from its due share of the commercial, industrial, and colonial wealth of nineteenth-century Britain as a whole, but it rarely emerges as integral to the wealth-making process. Money-making generally goes on elsewhere, but fiscal policy, banking, speculation in shares, investment overseas, and, above all, the basic need to *earn* money are a real enough concern of many of Trollope's most prominent characters. That most quintessential of all his gentlemen, Plantagenet Palliser, is insistent in Chapter 25 of *Can You Forgive Her?* that 'a desire for wealth is the source of all progress' and that civilization 'comes from what men call greed' (*CYFH* 262). This future Chancellor of the Exchequer and Prime Minister significantly adds, however, that 'mercenary tendencies' should properly be combined with honesty, and honesty is precisely the virtue that Trollope most readily associates with gentlemanliness. It is the gentlemanly virtues which redeem Palliser's England from the venality and unrestrained commercialism rife in the City of London and in manufacture alike. What most characterizes the society represented in Trollope's novels is its interrelatedness and not its deference. The old gentlemanly ruling class, rather than expressing a fastidious indifference to 'trade' and to money-making in general, is seen as setting the ideal, high moral standards which permit a larger nation to flourish both morally and economically. Although, as we have seen, Trollope sees realist fiction as challenging and exposing the inherent problems in any representation of ideals, it is nevertheless to the loosely defined values of the old gentlemanly class that he repeatedly and confidently returns.

The idea of the gentleman was under threat in Victorian England.[6] As Plantagenet Palliser puts it in Chapter 8 of *The Duke's Children*, the word 'gentleman' had become 'too vague to carry with it any meaning' (*DC* 67). Palliser may be specifically referring to the impropriety of a 'mere' gentleman's aspiring to marry the daughter of a duke, but he was putting his finger on a real contemporary problem of definition. From the evidence of Trollope's novels it was probably easier to tell who *wasn't* a gentleman rather than who self-evidently *was*. The problem of definition had been accentuated by the very expansion of the bourgeoisie and the professional classes on which the Victorians so prided themselves. The old nobility, represented by the Pallisers, knew where it stood and precisely who was numbered amongst it. The old, titleless gentry, by contrast, had developed into an amorphous caste, no longer exclusively landed, county based, interconnected by marriage, or armigerous and no longer defined on its outer edges by the gentlemanly professions: the church, medicine, the law, or the military. As the anonymous writer of *The Habits of Good Society: A Handbook of Etiquette for Ladies and Gentlemen* wrote in the 1850s:

> What does the middle-class mean? Not twenty years ago, it was taken to represent only the better portion of the commercial and lower half of professional society. I will remember with what a sneer some people spoke of a merchant, and the gulf that the barrister and physician asserted to exist between them and the lawyer and general practitioner. And how is it now? How many gentlemen of old family would now decline an introduction to a well-educated merchant... the middle-class has an enormous extent now, and even

> the landed gentry, when brought to town, mingle freely and gladly with commerce and the professions.[7]

An often impoverished gentry, long open to new recruitment from the merchant class, or from the upwardly mobile and educated, was now being swamped by large numbers of men and women with no definable 'family' but with a great deal of money, education, and influence. Some members of this pushy new class, such as Elizabeth Gaskell's self-assured Mr Thornton in *North and South* or the independently minded Polly Neefit in Trollope's *Ralph the Heir*, were simply not interested in acquiring the status and claims of gentility (and would have eschewed the use of guides to etiquette). Many others, such as Polly Neefit's rich breeches-maker of a father, aspired to lose the associations of 'trade' by gaining admittance to the gentlemanly class through a mutually advantageous marriage. Certain old snobberies remained in force, however. Lucius Mason in *Orley Farm* is, for example, determined not be an engineer because 'civil engineers were only tradesmen of an upper class, tradesmen with intellects' (*OF* i. 23). The narrator of *The Prime Minster* opens the novel with an expression of his own concern with what was shifting in the class structures and the class-definitions of Victorian Britain:

> It is certainly of service to a man to know who were his grandfathers and who were his grandmothers if he entertain an ambition to move in the upper circles of society, and also of service to be able to speak of them as of persons who were themselves somebodies in their time. No doubt we all entertain great respect for those who by their own energies have raised themselves in the world; and when we hear that the son of a washerwoman has become Lord Chancellor or Archbishop of Canterbury we do, theoretically and abstractly, feel a higher reverence for such self-made magnate than for one who has been as it were born into forensic or ecclesiastical purple. But not the less must the offspring of the washerwoman have had very much trouble on the subject of his birth, unless he has been, when young as well as when old, a very great man indeed. After the goal has been absolutely reached, and the honour and the titles and the wealth actually won, a man may talk with some humour, even with some affection, of the maternal tub; – but while the struggle is going on, with the conviction strong upon the struggler that he cannot be altogether successful unless he be esteemed a gentleman, not to be ashamed, not to conceal the old family circumstances, not at any rate to be silent, is difficult. (*PM* i. 1–2)

This passage, leading into the introduction of the shifty Ferdinand Lopez, needs to be read with a certain irony. The narrator goes on to insist that Lopez is admitted 'on all sides' to be a 'gentleman' (the word being in inverted commas). 'It was not generally believed that Ferdinand Lopez was well born,' he tells us, 'but he was a gentleman' even though it was understood that he 'did business in the City' (*PM* i. 3). By both insisting too much and by appearing to hedge his bets the narrator manages to convey the impression that, even before the novel's action begins, Lopez may prove to be that most ungentlemanly of creatures, a pushy cad.

When the narrator of *The Prime Minster* refers to humbly born potential lord chancellors and archbishops he knows that such historic promotions had come to pass (as the careers of Lord Eldon or Cardinal Wolsey might have served to prove), and that, unlike its continental neighbours, England had never legally defined rank. He also knows that class barriers and distinctions simply did not have their ancient authority in nineteenth-century England (they had never mattered so much in Scotland). He also seems to suspect that the future will deliver a process of yet more radical democratization. As we have already seen, however, Trollope himself remained wary about the evolutionary social process. Certainly, relatively few of his admirable characters are of obscure or ungenteel birth. This is particularly evident when it comes to his clergymen, the only exception being Henry Lovelace, the dean of Brotherton Cathedral in *Is He Popenjoy?* (the Dean's origins are in 'trade', as were Trollope's own maternal grandfather's). The odious and ambitious Obadiah Slope in *Barchester Towers* is, however, more of a Trollopian norm. Slope, we are wryly told, may just possibly be descended from Sterne's Dr Slop, but his family was still poor enough for him to have been merely a sizar at Cambridge and he has succeeded in his career only thanks to the patronage of Mrs Proudie. The much affronted Archdeacon Grantly will later wonder as to how he came to be ordained at all and snootily to demand: 'Did you ever see any animal less like a gentleman' (*BT* 43). The priggish evangelical Samuel Prong in *Rachel Ray* is a 'devout, good man ... sincere, hard-working, sufficiently intelligent ... but deficient in one vital qualification for a clergyman of the Church of England; he was not a gentleman' (*RR* 77).

Another low-born evangelical, the unscrupulous Irishman Jeremiah Maguire in *Miss Mackenzie* (1865), is dismissed by a lawyer as 'one of those fellows for whom nothing is too dirty'. 'Clergymen are like women,' he adds, 'as long as they're pure, they're a long sight purer than other men; but when they fall, they sink deeper' (*MM* 319).

Trollope's two baptized Jewish clergymen are both singularly far from being gentlemen. Certainly neither acts as such and both contrive to sink particularly deeply. Joseph Groschut, the Bishop of Brotherton's chaplain in *Is He Popenjoy?*, is ultimately banished from the cathedral because of conduct unbecoming with the daughter of a Low Church bookseller. Far more villainous is Joseph Emilius, born Yosef Mealyus in Prague, who figures prominently in both *The Eustace Diamonds* and *Phineas Redux*. In the former novel Emilius is a popular evangelical preacher who has 'come up quite suddenly' and whose pulpit oratory has attracted the benign notice of Lizzie Eustace. She finally marries him, though the match is greeted with disdain amongst the Pallisers (Lady Glencora dismisses Emilius as a cad and 'a Bohemian Jew . . . an imposter who has come over here to make a fortune' (*ED* ii. 373)). As we learn in *Phineas Redux*, Lizzie has left him within a year, leaving him with half her fortune. He is finally exposed as a bigamist and sent to prison (though the strong suspicion that he is also Mr Bonteen's murderer remains unproved).

Both Groschut and Emilius are regarded in 'society' as pushy, ungentlemanly, un-British frauds. It should not, however, be adduced that Trollope necessarily shared the snobbish anti-Semitism rife in Victorian England as a whole. His narrator in *Rachel Ray* renders ridiculous the popular prejudices against a Jewish candidate in a country election; the thoroughly admirable Madame Max Goesler (who figures prominently in the Palliser novels) is the widow of a Viennese Jewish banker, and one of his most eminent and learned lawyers, Solomon Aram in *Orley Farm*, is much admired by his gentile co-professionals ('You couldn't have a better man than old Solomon Aram' (*OF* i. 345)). Even in *The Way We Live Now*, Trollope's most extended critique of the decline of 'gentlemanly' standards in public life, the moral, financial, and social corruption associated with Augustus Melmotte is sharply contrasted with the uprightness and delicacy of the Jewish Banker, Ezekiel Breghert ('He was an honest man' (*WWLN* ii. 275)). As *The Way We Live Now* amply demonstrates, however, Trollope associates the decline of proper values in society with financial speculation, with mercenary principles, and with the determination of social outsiders, both native and foreign born, to become insiders. That the role of 'outsider' should be so frequently filled in Trollope's novels by Jewish entrepreneurs, moneylenders, speculators, and opportunists is testimony to both the new vitality of the Jewish presence in Victorian England and the ambiguity of Victorian gentile responses to that vitality.[8]

Trollope's Jewish characters, in common with many of his foreigners, tend to fail the 'gentleman' test because they cannot be readily 'placed' in social terms. They are essentially 'new' and, like the new urban industrial middle class, they appear to be unrooted. The foreign birth of an Emilius or a Melmotte, like an absence of socially established grandparents, counts against them. Money, intelligence, tact, and style make up for much, as the highly successful social career of Madame Max Goesler goes to prove, but, as Ferdinand Lopez discovers, the 'outsiderliness' remains as much of a drawback as a lack of birth and family. Melmotte, like his Romantic cognate, Maturin's Melmoth, is essentially a wanderer when it comes to British perceptions of class and status. Yet even for an Italian aristocrat, such as the wife of the Marquis of Brotherton in *Is He Popenjoy?*, a certain upper-class disdain dictates an 'infinite contempt ... for foreign nobility not of the highest order' (*IHP* i. 128).

In one highly significant instance, however, a degree of 'outsiderliness' appears to work professional and political wonders. Phineas Finn is the son of an Irish country doctor and a Catholic. He is not a foreigner, of course, but he has sprung from outside the *English* class system and from outside *English* patterns of kinship, friendship, and connection. Finn is initially alien to the establishment, but he is nevertheless enabled, given the party politics and the party compromises of Victorian England, to work subtly and successfully within it and on its behalf. Despite his native Catholicism, Phineas has been educated at the Anglican Trinity College, Dublin, and has been called to the English rather than the Irish bar. He chooses to stand as an MP for a predominantly Catholic seat in Co. Galway, defeating an Orangeman in the process, but, as his party perceives him, he is the opposite of 'a cantankerous, red-hot semi-Fenian' (*PF* i. 6). He is a stalwart Liberal, a member of the Reform Club, and, despite his ostensible lack of 'family', readily accepted as a gentleman. He also conspicuously thinks of himself as a 'Briton'. Trollope certainly does not give him a charmed political career, but, as we learn from the four novels in which he appears, he will variously serve in a series of Liberal cabinets as a Junior Lord of the Treasury, Under-Secretary for the Colonies, Chancellor of the Duchy of Lancaster, Secretary for the Colonies, Chief Secretary for Ireland, and First Lord of the Admiralty. Phineas finally achieves domestic happiness through a marriage to that other generous-spirited and socially accepted 'outsider', Madame Max.

The character of Phineas Finn was evidently shaped by Trollope's particular response to the society and the Unionist politics of nineteenth-century Ireland. He seems also to have conceived of him as a true gentleman. His influential presence in Trollope's political novels leads us inevitably back to the question of how the novelist himself defined 'gentlemanliness'. From the evidence of his fiction it would seem that Trollope placed a greater stress on manners than on birth, though he will never attempt to deny that the very fact of being well born is likely to have shaped and conditioned behaviour. He would probably have happily endorsed Cardinal Newman's celebrated suggestion that 'it is almost a definition of a gentleman, to say he is one who never inflicts pain', a suggestion that Newman expands on by arguing that a gentleman 'may be represented as one who... aims at others obtaining without his giving, at offering without obtruding, and at being felt without being seen'.[9] Trollope appears to be most affronted when certain of his high-born characters either insult or somehow misuse those who deserve more honourable treatment. He means his readers to be shocked when the Marquis of Brotherton dismisses his sister-in-law as 'that young w[hore]' in *Is He Popenjoy?* (IHP ii. 90). Not only does he refuse to print the word in full, he also seems to relish Dean Lovelace's angry assault on the man who has maligned his daughter's reputation. The narrator of *The Vicar of Bullhampton* is equally disturbed by the gross arrogance of the Marquis of Trowbridge, a man whose misuse of his noble inheritance is criticized at his very introduction to readers: 'His countenance would not have been bad, had not the weight of his marquisate always been there; nor would his heart have been bad, had it not been similarly burdened.' The marquis is 'a silly, weak, ignorant man, whose own capacity would hardly have procured bread for him in any trade or profession, had bread not been so adequately provided for him by his fathers before him' *(VB* 118). Adolphus Longstaffe, the squire of Caversham in *The Way We Live Now,* has an equal lack of generosity and shares a parallel arrogance:

> He was intensely proud of his position in life, thinking himself to be immensely superior to all those who earned their bread. There were no doubt gentlemen of different degrees, but the English gentleman of gentlemen was he who had land, and family title-deeds, and an old family place, and family portraits, and family embarrassments, and a family absence of any usual employment...He was a silly man, who had no fixed idea that it behoved him to be of any use to any one...There was very little that his position called upon him to do, but there was much that it forbad him to do. (*WWLN* i. 116–17)

When another genteel Adolphus, the socially ambitious Adolphus Crosbie, jilts Lily Dale in order to marry Lady Alexandrina de Courcy in *The Small House at Allington,* Trollope's narrator explodes with a rare expression of anger:

> It was a vile letter to have written – not because the language was bad, or the mode of expression unfeeling, or the facts falsely stated – but because the thing to be told was in itself so vile. There are deeds which will not bear a gloss – sins as to which the perpetrator cannot speak otherwise than as a reptile; circumstances which change a man and put upon him the worthlessness of vermin. (*SHA* 297)

It is small wonder that the world at large applauds when the worthy Johnny Eames pursues Crosbie and knocks him down in a bruising fight.

The contrast between the poor but honest Johnny Eames and the poor, ambitious, and unworthy Adolphus Crosbie points to a clear distinction between a gentleman who acts like a gentleman and a gentleman who turns out to be a cad. The one acts honourably according to an accepted social code; the other pursues a selfish, inconsiderate, and dishonest line of action which betrays the very idea of gentlemanliness. In Chapter 44 of

The Three Clerks Trollope's narrator draws a clear distinction between a working-class villain, Dickens's Bill Sikes, and his own unprincipled swindler, Undecimus Scott, the eleventh son of Lord Gaberlunzie:

> Bill could not boast the merit of selecting the course which he had run; he had served the Devil, having had, as it were, no choice in the matter; he was born and bred and educated an evil-doer, and could hardly have deserted from the colours of his great Captain, without some spiritual interposition to enable him to do so. To Undy a warmer reward must surely be due: he had been placed fairly on the world's surface, with power to choose between good and bad, and had deliberately taken the latter; to him had, at any rate, been explained the theory of *meum* and *tuum*, and he had resolved that he liked *tuum* better than *meum*; he had learnt that there is a God ruling over us, and a Devil hankering after us, and had made up his mind that he would belong to the latter. (*TC* 517)

Undy Scott merits the greater authorial punishment, not because he has fallen from the greater height, but because his birth and education permitted him to make choices. He has failed to act like the gentleman he was born to be. In just such a way the novelist lets us see that certain of his women characters, most notably Ladies Eustace and Mason, behave not just immorally by telling lies, but in a socially destructive way. Trollope attempts, therefore, to hold up an ideal of gentlemanly (and ladylike) conduct before his readers, though as a knowing novelist, he acknowledges that the ideal is frequently betrayed by those, both men and women, who should have been conditioned to act from a sense of honour rather than self-interest.

For Trollope the maintenance of an honourable, 'gentlemanly' code of conduct was essential to both the political and the commercial well-being of Great Britain. It was code, or rather an ethic, which gave the well born and the well educated a moral privilege which they squandered to the detriment of society as a whole. This ethic was much more than chivalry, or simple politeness, or a pattern of behaviour which could be learned from an etiquette book; it was a socially enabling morality. Trollope's idea of 'gentlemanliness' is at once intensely moral and flexible, a matter of high principles and leadership. Trollope's England is not divided into two hostile camps ignorant either of one another's 'habits, thoughts and feelings' or of one another's morals, manners, and intentions. As we observe it from Trollope's authorial perspective, it is a nation which is struggling to map out the nature of a new moral high ground which is no longer the exclusive preserve of those born to wealth and name. His England may not yet have dispensed with class distinctions and class snobberies, but his novels suggest that it is a nation in which its dominant middle class is subtly and morally evolving according to two crucial Darwinian principles – those of survival and adaptability.

4

Trollope and Politics

Despite the much vaunted claim that the British Parliament enjoys an 800-year history, much that is essential in the British understanding of how its Parliament works and what and who its Parliament represents is a relatively recent creation. Much indeed came into being in Anthony Trollope's lifetime. The Westminster Parliament had been 'British' only since the Act of Union with Scotland in 1707. Irish members sat in it only when a similar Act of Union in 1801 had abolished Ireland's separate legislative body. This 'imperial' Parliament became representative of the diversity of the British people as a whole only by means of a steady campaign of reform introduced as the nineteenth century advanced. Protestant Dissenters were given full civil rights in 1828, Roman Catholics in 1829. The great Reform Act of 1832 allotted seats to most of the new industrial cities of the Midlands and the north for the first time and extended the franchise to a new, and predominantly urban, section of the middle class. It had also, supposedly, abolished 'rotten boroughs' such as the fictional one which had formerly been sold 'at every election to the highest bidder on his side' (*VB* 3) by the Marquis of Trowbridge in *The Vicar of Bullhampton*. The further Reform Acts of 1867 and 1882 gradually brought most of the male working class into the democratic process. Finally, the pressure to extend the suffrage to women (granted partially in 1918 and fully only in 1922) formed one of the great political debates of the second half of the Victorian age (the debate figures, somewhat flippantly, in *Is He Popenjoy?*). Most of the old Palace of Westminster, the historic seat of the two Houses of Parliament, had burned to the ground in 1834 and had been replaced in the middle decades of the nineteenth century by the superb Gothic fantasy designed by Barry and Pugin. Although the medieval style and the complex scheme of decoration for its interiors stressed the idea of a long and continuous history for Parliament, the new building was also an emphatic statement of the Victorian concept of representative government, representative that is both of the Union and of the expanding and often disparate electorate of that Union.

Trollope's concern with politics, and with the meaning of politics, is by no means confined to the functions and malfunctions of parliamentary democracy. The dominant focus of his novels on provincial upper- and middle-class England not only allows him to explore the wider social ramifications of the workings of the two Houses of Parliament beyond the confines of Westminster; it also gives him the opportunity of observing local reflections of, and alternatives to, national 'high' politics. Unlike many twentieth-century commentators, he does not understand politics in terms of mass movements, of class conflict, or of popular or populist causes. As with his relatively narrow representation of class, he is substantially preoccupied with the affairs of the Victorian 'ruling class'. This 'ruling class' is made up of those with a traditional access to political power structures in Britain. His aristocrats, such as the Pallisers, have a base in the House of Lords as well as influence over the Commons through their surviving 'pocket boroughs' in rural Barsetshire. Trollope's gentry and professional classes, descendants of those who had for centuries dominated both the electorate and the membership of the Commons, tend to uphold the noble principle that 'it is the highest and most legitimate pride of an Englishman to have the letters M.P. written after his name, (*CYFH* ii. 44). Yet, as Trollope consistently observes, England and the wider United Kingdom were changing and adapting as times and conditions evolved.

One vital aspect of the delineation of politics in Trollope's novels is his early fascination with the internal politics of the true 'Establishment', the Church of England. Long seen as an arm of the English state, which determined its formularies and appointed its bishops, the Church of England had inevitably succumbed to the campaign of reform evolved by Whig governments in the 1830s and which was assumed to be a hallmark of Liberal party policy from the 1850s onwards. This had in turn provoked the protest, subsequently known as the

Oxford Movement, which both insistently explored the Church's catholic roots and opened the way for an administrative revolution in its affairs.[1] Trollope's Barsetshire churchmen know that they are confronted with changes which either they choose to resist or they determine to waylay. This is a situation which still most readily evokes the use of the adjective 'Trollopian'. Trollope's Church remains dominated by bishops appointed to act in the House of Lords as willing political tools. The inconvenient death of Dr Grantly in the opening chapter of *Barchester Towers* takes place 'exactly as the ministry of Lord – was going to give place to that of Lord – . . . and it became . . . a matter of intense interest to those concerned whether the new appointment should be made by a conservative or liberal government' (*BT* 1). Despite the fact that he had been described in *The Warden* as 'a bland and kind old man, opposed by every feeling to authoritative demonstration and episcopal ostentation', the worldly Dr Grantly has commanded a yearly income of £9,000, has amassed considerable wealth for his only son, and has appointed that son to the influential post of Archdeacon of Barchester (as well as to the 'plum' living of Plumstead Episcopi).[2] Bishop Grantly was a prelate of the old school, precisely the kind of bishop looked on with disfavour both by reforming governments and by earnest and radical clerics of the 1850s. His Tory son, who has effectively run the diocese, and who is far from averse to worldly ambition, is not promoted in his place. Like many able men, the Archdeacon believes that he would have imparted a becoming dignity to a position which, because of something akin to political correctness, has been given to a less worthy man. What Barchester gets, and generally resents, is Bishop Proudie, appointed by a Liberal government because he had 'become known as a useful and rising clergyman' who 'early in life adapted himself to the views held by the whigs on most theological and religious subjects' (*BT* 18, 19) (he has also proved to be 'useful' on government commissions). His income has also been cut to £5,000 by recent legislation. Proudie's chief impediment, in the eyes both of his creator and of the Barchester clergy, is his formidable wife, for, as the narrator of *The Last Chronicle of Barset* wryly comments, 'He might have been a sufficiently good bishop, had it not been that Mrs Proudie was so much more than a sufficiently good bishop's wife' (*LCB* 870). Apart from this singular incumbrance, Proudie is a decent enough man and, in his way, an effective bishop. He may lack the easy diplomatic skills of the local diocesan in *The Vicar of Bullhampton*, but he is in many ways not far from the bland ideal embodied in that other major Trollopian prelate, the Bishop of Elmham in *The Way We Live Now*. As the narrator tells us:

> Among the poor around him he was idolized, and by such clergy of his diocese as were not enthusiastic in their theology either on the one side or on the other, he was regarded as a model bishop ... He was an unselfish man, who loved his neighbour as himself, and forgave all trespasses, and thanked God for his daily bread from his heart, and prayed heartily to be delivered from temptation. But I doubt whether he was competent to teach a creed, – or even to hold one, if it be necessary that a man should understand and define his creed before he can hold it. (*WWLN* i. 148–9)

The narrator of *The Way We Live Now* knows that the quintessentially liberal and broad-church Bishop of Elmham does not please those of his clergy who are 'enthusiastic in their theology'. This he explains as those who are divided in their churchmanship between the 'very high' and the 'very low', those who regarded ritualism 'as being either heavenly or devilish'. Trollope is touching here on the great controversy which had begun to divide the Church of England in the 1830s and which continued to vex it forty years later. The Oxford Movement, and its progeny of catholic-minded clergy, known variously as 'Puseyites', 'Tractarians', or latterly as 'Ritualists', willingly saw themselves both as heirs to the old 'High-Church' tradition and as divided by a fixed gulf from the 'Low-Church' party (now often identified with Evangelicalism). As disagreements were often fundamental, there was little love lost between the two parties. Whereas Trollope seems to have found ritualism merely eccentric, and moderate tractarianism generally admirable, his evangelicals are uniformly odious.[3] The fact that Mrs Proudie is a patron of strict sabbatarians and teetotallers does not render her particularly agreeable to his urbane clerics. Her creator offers a minimal apologia for her in *An Autobiography*:

> she was a tyrant, a bully, a would-be priestess, a very vulgar woman, and one who would send headlong to the nethermost pit all who

> disagreed with her; – but...she was conscientious, by no means a hypocrite, really believing in the brimstone which she threatened – and anxious to save the souls around her from its horrors. (*A*. 177)

Nevertheless her essential 'vulgarity' links her directly to that line of low-born evangelical clergymen who, as we have already noted, generally prove themselves to be out and out hypocrites. A related narrow-minded and destructive vulgarity infects the *Christian Examiner*, the weekly newspaper of Low-Church Littlebath in *Miss Mackenzie* and determines the censorious attitudes of the Reverend Samuel Prong and his disciple, Mrs Prime, in *Rachel Ray*. If we are to judge by the Reverend Francis Arabin, however, Trollope's moderate High-Churchmen seem, by contrast, to be scholars, gentlemen, and benign, historically minded reformers. Arabin, successively a Fellow of Lazarus College, Oxford, Vicar of St Ewold's, and Dean of Barchester, is 'a poet, a polemical writer...and eloquent clergyman, a droll, odd humorous, energetic, conscientious man...[and] a thorough gentleman'. Having formerly accepted the enforced celibacy of an Oxford don, Arabin happily woos and marries Eleanor Bold once he has established himself in Barchester. He has also, we are told, been happily delivered from a worse fate, for when 'Mr Newman left the Church of England [on his conversion to Roman Catholicism in 1845]...he did not carry off Mr Arabin, but the escape which that gentleman had was a very narrow one' (*BT* 188–9).

Despite their Anglican bias, Trollope's novels reveal little obvious antagonism between Anglican and Roman Catholic clergy. His first novel, *The Macdermots of Ballycloran*, has an Irish Catholic priest as its hero; his third, *La Vendee*, gives prominence to the admirable Father Jerome; in the short humorous story 'Father Giles of Ballymoy' the title character emerges as the type of generous-minded Irishman that Trollope most admired, and, in *An Eye for an Eye* the upright Irish priest, Father Marty, is treated with considerable respect. But then none of the four priests is English. Trollope's most prominent English Catholic clergyman is the gentlemanly convert, Father John Barham, an Oxford graduate and an impoverished but determined proselytizer. If anything, Barham is more of a social embarrassment than a threat to his antagonists. The Bishop of Elmham appears assured enough when he and his wife discuss their recent encounter. Mrs Yeld is clearly offended by Barham's arguments:

> '...Of course I don't want to be prejudiced, but Protestants are Protestants, and Roman Catholics are Roman Catholics.'
>
> 'You may say the same of Liberals and Conservatives, but you wouldn't have them decline to meet each other.'
>
> 'It isn't quite the same, my dear. After all religion is religion.'
>
> 'It ought to be,' said the bishop.
>
> 'Of course, I don't mean to put myself up against you, my dear, but I don't know that I want to meet Mr Barham again.'
>
> 'I don't know that I do, either,' said the bishop, 'but if he comes in my way I hope I shall treat him civilly.' (*WWLN* i. 156)

As the Yelds recognize, English religion and English politics remain inextricably bound together, though not perhaps with the anti-Catholic fervour that had marked them in the seventeenth and eighteenth centuries. A far more damaging religio-political antagonism appears to exist between Anglicans and Dissenters. Dissenters now carried considerable weight in provincial politics and continued to bear a grudge against the Anglican establishment which had once, through Acts of Parliament, discriminated against them. The Conservative Mrs Tregear in *The Duke's Children* fears the election of 'a godless dissenter' as the representative of a Cornish borough, while her husband insists that 'we used ... to endeavour to get someone to represent us in Parliament, who would agree with us on vital subjects, such as the Church of England and the necessity of religion' (*DC* i. 437). In *Ralph the Heir* the would-be Conservative MP Sir Thomas Underwood is obliged to canvas the Methodist minister of Percycoss, Pabsby (whose voice is made up 'of pretence, politeness and saliva' (*RH* i. 246)), because Methodists are both 'respectable' and generally more inclined to the reformist Liberals (Pabsby conspicuously does not vote for him). In *The Vicar of Bullhampton*, however, the Marquis of Trowbridge exploits the ambitions of the Methodist minister of Bullhampton by provocatively building a new red-brick chapel in full view of the vicarage. It is a gesture designed both to spite the vicar and to exploit historic tensions between the Establishment and those who, like the Methodists, were insistently proud of their religious independence. On a far more petty level, when in *Doctor Thorne* the amorous Miss Gushing is rejected by her tellingly named rector, the Reverend Caleb Oriel, she joins the

Primitive Methodists in a pique and then proceeds to marry the equally tellingly named minister, Mr Rantaway.

The disestablishment of the Church of England is the (unsuccessful) political issue discussed in *Phineas Redux*, though the matter often seems as whimsical in terms of contemporary politics as Plantagenet Palliser's aim of introducing a decimal currency. What truly fascinates Trollope about everyday politics in the early Barchester novels is not how the State interrelates with the Church but how the devices and desires of a tightly knit group of upper clergymen (and their spouses) can be seen to mirror the manœuvres of metropolitan statesmen. Despite his sincere, private professions of Anglican Christian belief, Trollope remains a remarkably secular novelist. As he remarks of Archdeacon Grantly in *Framley Parsonage*, 'he was a man who knew how to fight his battles among men – sometimes without too close a regard to his cloth' (*FP* 544). Mr Harding's loss of his wardenship and the fall of Obadiah Slope will be reflected in those later novels which touch on the making and unmaking of governments and on the vagaries of parliamentary careers. In a significant sense, *The Warden* can be seen as Trollope's earliest *political* novel, in that it explores how a local problem can be blown up into a national one and how the general spirit of reform, so prevalent in mid-Victorian life, can disrupt the staid and privileged rhythms of provincial life. *The Warden* is also the first of Trollope's novels to explore the new power of the press in influencing both motives and events. When Mr Harding's problems at Hiram's Hospital become the subject of a measured editorial in the *Jupiter* (Trollope's name for *The Times*), what was once a provincial scandal becomes a national one. Harding finds himself held up as an unhappy representative of the Church's 'moral indifference':

> They say that eighty thousand copies of the *Jupiter* are daily sold, and that each copy is read by five persons at the least. Four hundred thousand readers then would hear this accusation against him, four hundred thousand hearts would swell with indignation at the griping injustice, the barefaced robbery of the warden of Barchester Hospital! And how was he to answer this? How was he to open his inmost heart to this multitude, to these thousands, the educated, the polished, the picked men of his own country; how show them that he was no robber, no avaricious, lazy priest scrambling for gold, but

> a retiring, humble-spirited man who had innocently taken what had innocently been offered to him? (W. 91–2)

Harding is the first fictional victim of a sententious and bullying press, and later of an avowedly populist and propagandist literature (represented by Dr Pessimist Anticant and Mr Popular Sentiment). His little, local nineteenth-century difficulty would, however, have been magnified many times in twentieth-century Britain by an impatient, smugly self-righteous, and unbridled media, the articulators of 'public opinion'.

What the retiring Mr Harding experiences at the hands of the *Jupiter* is only what a harder-edged Victorian politician or clergyman had come to expect of the contemporary press. It is the *Jupiter* which rightly speculates as to who the new bishop will be in *Barchester Towers* and it is an editorial in the *Jupiter* which helps bring about Mark Roberts's clerical nemesis in *Framley Parsonage*. In the same novel the brittle Harold Smith MP declares, as have many MPs since his time, that 'we are becoming the slaves of a mercenary and irresponsible press'. Smith goes on to insist that one *Jupiter* journalist in particular, Tom Towers, 'is able to overturn the Government and throw the whole country into dismay' (*FP* 269). It is an exaggeration, of course, but, as we see throughout the course of the novel, Towers and his newspaper rejoice in the pomposity of their denunciations of politicians (much as they had denounced Mr Harding). Towers may be the most prominent journalist in Trollope's novels, but his 'gentlemanliness', his legal training, and, as his name indicates, his Oxford education redeem him from being the most unpleasant and self-seeking. That dubious distinction is reserved for Quintus Slide, the young and aggressive editor of the *People's Banner* and the type of a new breed of newspaperman emerging in the 1860s. Slide drops his aitches, writes good English 'with great rapidity, and was possessed of that special sort of political fervour which shows itself in a man's work rather than in his conduct' (W. 91–2). He is also an early master of what is now called the 'exposé'. He first appears in *Phineas Finn*, initially espouses Finn's cause, but turns on him and proves himself his bitter enemy in that novel and in its sequel. Having attempted to invite himself to Gatherum Castle in *The Prime Minister* (and having been refused), he also takes publicly against the Duke of Omnium, finally rejoicing both in the fall of the Duke's administration and in his exclusion from the successor government ('The editor had no hesitation in declaring that he, by his own sagacity and persistency, had made certain the exclusion of that very unfit and pressing candidate for office' (*PM* ii. 363)).

Slide's campaign against the Duke in *The Prime Minister* is centred on exploiting the unhappy consequences of the Duchess's great *faux pas* in seeming to support Ferdinand Lopez's candidacy in the Silverbridge election. But then the Duchess had always delighted in intrigue, both in politics and in her emotional life (it makes for a particularly stormy marriage, as the Palliser novels as a whole serve to suggest). What Trollope also highlights in describing in the Duchess's manœuvres is the behind-the-scenes power exercised by political wives. Still excluded from direct participation in the party-political processes of British democracy, well-placed women were none the less able to influence events and appointments through their dinner parties, receptions, and country weekends. Lady Glencora as the Duchess of Omnium brings the hospitable resources of both Gatherum Castle and the significantly named Matching Priory fully into play in furthering her husband's career. As she declares on his appointment to the premiership in *The Prime Minister*, 'if I can only do anything I will slave for you', later adding as an assertive society hostess: 'I should like to make Buckingham Palace second rate' (*PM* i. 54–5). In one sense what she does parallels the 'interfering' Mrs Proudie; in another, readily appreciated by Victorian readers, she is doing what would properly be expected of a woman in her position. Bishops' wives were assumed to be merely self-effacing hostesses; political wives were generally considered to be far more integral to the broad political process, albeit discreetly.

Political hostesses such as the Duchess and Madame Max Goesler function in a world where the old aristocracy still contrives to dominate the political life of Victorian Britain. It is a fictional world in which the Pallisers, the St Bungays, and the De Courcys stand in for the real one of the Russells, the Cavendishes, and the Cecils. But it is also a world of political expediency, one in which new, or convenient, men rise and are blessed in their rise. Although considerable ingenuity has gone into identifying Trollopian stand-ins for Lord John Russell (Mr

Mildmay), Derby (Lord de Terrier), Palmerston (Lord Brock), Disraeli (Sidonia and Mr Daubeny), and Gladstone (Mr Finespun and Mr Gresham), the novelist himself always insisted that he was drawing portraits 'not of living men, but of living political characters' (*A.* 227).[4] He is generally at his best describing individual (and fictional) politicians rather than administrations and he draws these men from a variety of backgrounds. Phineas Finn has, as we have seen, the advantage of Irish and Catholic roots. The radical Mr Monk, who, when we first meet him in *Phineas Finn,* has 'devoted his whole life to politics hitherto without any personal reward beyond that which came to him from the reputation of his name, and from the honour of a seat in Parliament', has four brothers 'all in trade' (*PF* i. 128). Mr Bott, who makes himself so useful to the Palliser cause in Parliament and beyond it, proves to be odious to Lady Glencora partly because he 'comes out of Lancashire, and made calico' (*CYFH* i. 241). When her husband loses power in *The Prime Minister,* Lady Glencora dismisses Bott as 'vulgar' and as 'one of the arithmetical men', and expresses a bitter delight at the prospect of leaving 'ministerial supporters' behind her and returning to the company of 'ladies and gentlemen' (*PM* ii. 300). Nevertheless, as two further Trollope novels suggest, the social complexion of the House of Commons had in fact changed sufficiently for Ontario Moggs (the son of a London bootmaker) to stand for Percycross in *Ralph the Heir,* and for the wealthy Jewish tailor, Mr Hart, to be a candidate for the borough of Butler Cornbury in *Rachel Ray.* They are both, significantly, radical Liberals.

It was to the new Liberal Party, then at its vigorous apogee, that Trollope gave his somewhat ambiguous loyalty. Although he described himself in *An Autobiography* as 'an advanced conservative Liberal' (*A.* 186), he claimed that he saw no 'absurdity' in the phrase and was sufficiently committed to the cause to stand in the Liberal interest at Beverley. He also freely admitted to having no defined political ideology:

> A man who entertains in his mind any political doctrine, except as a means of improving the condition of his fellows, I regard as a political intriguer, a charlatan, and a conjurer, – as one who thinks that by a certain amount of wary wire-pulling he may raise himself in the estimation of the world.
>
> I am aware that this theory of politics will seem to many to be

> stilted, overstrained, and, as the Americans would say, hi-foluting. (*A.* 188)

This bluntly anti-theoretic, anti-doctrinaire approach to contemporary politics tends to mark Trollope's generally tolerant observation of politics in action. As he had reason to know following the débâcle at Beverley, nineteenth-century elections did not necessarily reflect the quality either of the candidates in those elections or of the governments that subsequently emerged. Significantly enough, the manifold corruptions of the borough of Percycross, as they are described in *Ralph the Heir*, leave both the Conservative, Sir Thomas Underwood, and his radical opponent, Ontario Moggs, chastened and to some degree disillusioned with the existing state of representative government. Trollope's upright, principled, dutiful, and well-meaning politicians, and most notably Plantagenet Palliser, tend to suggest the potential of a far more optimistic Trollopian political analysis. But then, equally significantly, thanks to their rank and influence, none of the Pallisers ever has to run the gamut of truly popular politics.

Trollope's 'conservative Liberalism' certainly shapes the opinions both of his more admirable fictional politicians and of his narrators. At the opening of Chapter 54 of *The Way We Live Now*, for example, his narrator describes his perception of the established principles of the Conservative party in power:

> The Conservative party at this particular period was putting its shoulder to the wheel, – not to push the coach up any hill, but to prevent its being hurried along at a pace which was not only dangerous, but manifestly destructive. The Conservative party now and then does put its shoulder to the wheel, ostensibly with the great national object above named; but also actuated by a natural desire to keep its own head well above water and be generally doing something, so that other parties may not suppose that it is moribund. (*WWLN* ii. 31)

This is sharp enough, but when, later in the same chapter, Augustus Melmotte's Conservative candidacy in the Westminster by-election is introduced, the same narrator speaks with a due degree of cynicism about the motives both of the candidate and, by implication, of the party that has selected him:

> There was one man who thoroughly believed that the thing at the

> present moment most essentially necessary to England's glory was the return of Mr Melmotte for Westminster. This man was undoubtedly a very ignorant man. He knew nothing of any one political question which had vexed England for the last half century, – nothing whatever of the political history which had made England what it was at the beginning of that half century... He had not even reflected how a despotic monarch or a federal republic might affect himself, and possibly did not comprehend the meaning of those terms. But yet he was fully confident that England did demand and ought to demand that Mr Melmotte should be returned for Westminster. This man was Mr Melmotte himself. (*WWLN* ii. 34)

This passage may well have a peculiar resonance in the late twentieth century, cynical as that century has often become about the motives and morals of its politicians. What Trollope seems to be implying, however, is that Melmotte is a much more *probable* Victorian Conservative than he is a Victorian Liberal, having failed to grasp the great, but often vaguely defined, principle of evolutionary reform.

This is not to imply that Trollope saw the division between the Conservative and Liberal parties as ideological.[5] He is particularly ambivalent about party politics in *Phineas Finn* and *Phineas Redux*. In the latter novel the Duke of St Bungay describes party loyalty as a loose kind of tribalism, a 'devotion to the side which a man conceives to be his side, and which he cannot leave without danger to himself'. In *Phineas Finn* Barrington Erle expresses a horror about politicians with defined or individualistic principles:

> According to his theory of parliamentary government, the House of Commons should be divided by a marked line, and every member should be required to stand on one side of it or on the other... He thought that debates were good because of the people outside, – because they served to create that public opinion which was hereafter to be used in creating some future House of Commons, but he did not think it possible that any vote should be given on a great question, either this way or that, as the result of a debate; and he was certainly assured.. that any such changing of votes would be dangerous, revolutionary, and almost unparliamentary. A member's vote... was due to the leader of that member's party. Such was Mr Erle's idea of the English system of Parliament. (*PF* i. 17–19)

Trollope does not necessarily endorse this anti-idealistic theory, but he steadily acknowledges that it is a theory that holds in the actual practice of party politics. When, in *The Duke's Children*, Plantagenet Palliser's son, Lord Silverbridge, deserts the family's traditional Whig/Liberal allegiance for the Conservative Party, his father sees it as a betrayal more of ancestral loyalty than of political dogma or principle. The pliable voters in the family pocket borough of Silverbridge appear to agree.

Trollope's principled radicals, contained within the loose parameters of the Liberal Party, are, however, never portrayed as disagreeable. Indeed, in *Rachel Ray*, his narrator carefully and spiritedly defends Luke Rowan's radicalism:

> He was a radical at heart if ever there was a radical. But in saying this I must beg my reader to understand that a radical is not necessarily a revolutionist, or even a republican. He does not, by reason of his social or political radicalism, desire the ruin of thrones, the degradation of nobles, the spoliation of the rich, or even the downfall of the bench of bishops. Many a young man is frightened away from the just conclusions of his mind and the strong convictions of his heart by dread of being classed with those who are jealous of the favoured ones of fortune. A radical may be as ready as any aristocrat to support the Crown with his blood, and the Church with his faith. It is in this that he is a radical; that he desires, expects, works for, and believes in, the gradual progress of the people. (*RR* 340–1).

Ontario Moggs, whose father believes that he holds 'horrible ideas about co-operative associations, the rights of labour, and the welfare of the masses' in *Ralph the Heir*, writes in an elevated manner to his beloved Polly explaining that 'the honourable prospect of having a seat in the British House of Parliament' is 'the highest dignity that a Briton can enjoy' (*RH* 316). In this he differs little from the line of upright gentlemen who aspire to the same honour and dignity. It is nevertheless true that Trollope's more conservative Liberals have the edge on his radicals, and it is to them that he gives the best tunes.

Undoubtedly, the sweetest singer of those tunes is Trollope's quintessential gentleman, Plantagenet Palliser. It is he who is flatteringly described in *Can You Forgive Her?* as 'one of those politicians in possessing whom England has perhaps more reason to be proud than any other of her resources, and who, as a body, give to her that exquisite combination of conservatism and progress which is her present strength and best security for the future' (*CYFH* i. 246). In *The Prime Minister* Palliser, now the Duke of Omnium, defines the distinction between Conservatism and his own conception of Liberal rectitude:

> The Conservative who has had any idea of the meaning of the name which he carries, wishes, I suppose, to maintain the differences and the distances which separate the highly placed from their lower brethren. He thinks that God has divided the world as he finds it divided ... The doctrine of Liberalism is, of course, the reverse. The Liberal, if he have any fixed idea at all, must, I think, have conceived the idea of lessening distances, – of bringing the coachman and the duke nearer together, – nearer and nearer, till a millennium shall be reached. (*PM* ii. 264–5)

Palliser is not talking simply of equality, but of a Liberalism which strives for 'some nearer approach to equality', strives, that is, for an ideal which in its millennial perfection is 'unattainable'. As he speaks Palliser becomes so uncommonly enthusiastic that he throws off his hat and looks up 'among the clouds'. What Trollope seems to be exploring here and throughout the Palliser novels is his hero's political ambiguity, an ambiguity which he almost certainly shared. Both men are progressives, but gradualists. Both, too, are obliged to recognize inconsistencies in their conception of progress. In *The Duke's Children* Palliser proudly proclaims the propriety of a prime minister's power to create a duke and of a man raising himself to that dignity 'by his own intellect' (*DC* ii. 390), while, at the same time, unbendingly resisting the idea of his heir marrying an American and of his daughter allying herself with a poor commoner.[6] As the novel proves, however, progress, and the wilfulness of a younger generation, are to have their way and the Duke graciously bends to the inevitable, a gentleman to the last. Although the tale is alluded to several times, *The Duke's Children* never aspires to be a large-scale variation on the story of King Cophetua and the Beggarmaid. It is not a story of stooping *de haut en bas*, nor is it a parable based on the idea of *noblesse oblige*. It explores, as much of Trollope's best fiction does, the passage of time and the often painful wisdom that time and change usher in. Here, in the climactic novel of the six Palliser novels, the Duke bows privately to the progressive political and social principles to which he has publicly proclaimed his loyalty throughout his career. The millennium is not ushered in, nor are his children set fair to be harbingers of egalitarianism, but at the end of the novel society is seen to have edged unsteadily nearer the realization of that levelling millennium.

Trollope is essentially a novelist of the Victorian age. Neither in terms of his narrative techniques nor in terms of his ideas does he look directly forward to the innovations of the twentieth century. His conservatism and his radicalism, in matters political and matters literary, were both responses to the conditions he found in his lifetime. As a compulsive and assertive fox-hunter, as a firm believer in the patronage system, as a moral upholder of the idea of gentlemanliness, and as a staid and dogged 'realist', he often seems enmeshed in codes which may strike a modern reader as alien. Paradoxically, perhaps, he has probably found more sympathetic readers in the twentieth century than he ever did in the nineteenth, and he continues to draw them in large numbers. As the twentieth century closes, all of his fiction is in print and available in accessible, well-edited, and popularly priced editions. Although he still rarely appears on the syllabuses of university English courses, his works steadily outsell those of his more readily 'canonized' and analysed rivals and contemporaries. He is a prolific writer, but not a daunting one. He is a demanding writer, but not an arcane one. His genius lies in observing a particularly fertile and vibrant section of Victorian society, but, in describing what is essentially 'the way we lived then', he is often capable of provoking his readers into recognizing uncomfortable and disconcerting parallels with the way we live now.

Notes

CHAPTER 1. THE LIFE AND *AN AUTOBIOGRAPHY*

1. The best scholarly biography of Trollope is N. John Hall's *Trollope: A Biography* (Oxford: Clarendon Press, 1991). It is usefully supplemented by Victoria Glendenning's lively *Anthony Trollope* (London: Hutchinson, 1992).
2. Quoted by Victoria Glendenning, *Anthony Trollope* 182, 207.
3. The most recent biography of Frances Trollope is Pamela Neville-Singleton, *Fanny Trollope: The Life and Adventures of a Clever Woman* (London: Viking, 1997).
4. Anthony Trollope, 'Thackeray', *Cornhill* (Feb. 1864).
5. The suggestion is Ruth ap Roberts's, in *Trollope: Artist and Moralist* (London: Chatto & Windus, 1971), 167.
6. James's comment is quoted in N. John Hall, *Trollope*, 407. James's reviews of *Miss Mackenzie* (1865) and *The Belton Estate* (1866) are reprinted in Donald Smalley (ed.), *Trollope: The Critical Heritage* (London: Routledge & Kegan Paul, 1969). His warm tribute to Trollope's 'genius' appeared in the *Century Magazine* in June 1883, it was reprinted in *Partial Portraits* in 1888, and is reprinted in Smalley, *Trollope*, 525–45.

CHAPTER 2. TROLLOPE THE CRITIC AND HIS CONTEMPORARIES

1. *John Bull* (22 May 1847). Repr. in Donald Smalley (ed.), *Trollope: The Critical Heritage* (London: Routledge & Kegan Paul, 1969), 549.
2. Unsigned essay in *The Times*, 7 Dec. 1882; Richard Holt Hutton, 'From Miss Austen to Mr Trollope', *Spectator*, 16 Dec. 1882, both repr. in Smalley (ed.), *Trollope*, 502, 509.
3. Henry James, 'Anthony Trollope', *Century Magazine* (July 1883); repr. in *Partial Portraits* (1888) and Smalley (ed.), *Trollope*, 525–45.

4. Anthony Trollope, 'Charles Dickens', *Saint Pauls Magazine*, 6 (July 1870), 370–5, Trollope also referred to Dickens's 'want of art in the choice of words and want of nature in the creation of character'.
5. George Eliot, 'The Natural History of German Life' (July 1856), repr. in *Essays of George Eliot*, ed. Thomas Penney (London: Routledge & Kegan Paul, 1963).
6. See e.g. for 'pioneer' reassessments of Dickens's work, Humphry House, *The Dickens World* (Oxford: Oxford University Press, 1941), J. Hillis Miller, *Charles Dickens: The World of his Novels* (Cambridge, Mass., Harvard University Press, 1958), and Robert Garis, *The Dickens Theatre: A Reassessement of the Novels* (Oxford: Clarendon Press, 1965).
7. *The George Eliot Letters*, ed. G. S. Haight, (9 vols.; New Haven, Conn.: Yale University Press, 1954–78), iii. 360; iv. 59.
8. Ibid. iv. 8–9.
9. The remark, made to Eliza Lynn Linton, is quoted in T. H. S. Escott's *Anthony Trollope: His Work, Associates, and Literary Originals* (London: John Lane, 1913), 185.
10. These parallels were noted by the critic of the *Dublin Review* in October 1872. The review is reprinted in Smalley (ed.), *Trollope*, 361.
11. *The Letters of Mrs Gaskell*, ed. J. A. V. Chapple and Arthur Pollard (Manchester: Manchester University Press, 1966), 602.
12. For Trollope's approach to Thackeray and his work, see J. Hillis Miller, 'Trollope's Thackeray' (1982), repr. in *Victorian Subjects* (Durham, NC.: Duke University Press, 1991), 271–7, and Andrew Sanders, 'Trollope's *Thackeray*', *Trollopiana: The Journal of the Trollope Society*, 24 (Feb. 1994), 4–17.
13. For this idea, see Gordon N. Ray, *Thackeray: The Uses of Adversity* (London: Oxford University Press, 1955), 20.
14. George Meredith, *An Essay on Comedy and the Uses of the Comic Spirit* (London: Constable, 1896), 27.
15. For particularly informed and illuminating discussions of Trollope as a nineteenth-century realist, see David Skilton, *Anthony Trollope and his Contemporaries* (London: Longman, 1972), and Stephen Wall, *Trollope and Character* (London: Faber and Faber, 1988). Lilian Furst's interesting recent study *All is True: The Claims and Strategies of Realist Fiction* (Durham NC and London: Duke University Press, 1995) does not, alas, discuss either Trollope or Thackeray.

CHAPTER 3. TROLLOPE AND CLASS

1. Benjamin Disraeli, *Sybil: or the Two Nations*, ed. Thom Braun (Penguin Classics; Harmondsworth: Penguin, 1980), 96.

2. Karl Marx and Friedrich Engels, *The Communist Manifesto*, ed. David McLellan (World's Classics; Oxford University Press, Oxford: 1992), 3.
3. For the debate on these issues, see Keith Robbins, *Nineteenth-Century Britain: England, Scotland, and Wales: The Making of a Nation* (Oxford: Oxford University Press, 1988); F. M. L. Thompson, *The Rise of Respectable Society: A Social History of Victorian Britain, 1830–1900* (Oxford: Oxford University Press, 1988); Gareth Stedman Jones, *Languages of Class: Studies in English Working Class History 1832–1982* (Cambridge: Cambridge University Press, 1983), and Geoffrey Crossick, 'From Gentleman to the Residuum: Languages of Social Description in Victorian Britain', in Penelope J. Corfield (ed.), *Language, History and Class* (Oxford: Blackwell, 1991).
4. The best survey of 'condition-of-England' fiction remains Sheila M. Smith, *The Other Nation: The Poor in English Novels of the 1840s and 1850s* (Oxford: Oxford University Press, 1980).
5. For the shift away from the radicalism of the 1840s, see Thompson, *The Rise of Respectable Society*.
6. The subject has been explored in both Robin Gilmour, *The Idea of the Gentleman in the Victorian Novel* (London: Allen & Unwin, 1981), and Shirley Robin Letwin, *The Gentleman in Trollope: Individuality and Moral Conduct* (London: Macmillan, 1982). Martin J. Wiener, *English Culture and the Decline of the Industrial Spirit* (Cambridge: Cambridge University Press, 1981) and Lawrence Stone and Jeanne C. Fawtier Stone *An Open Elite: England 1540–1880* (Oxford: Clarendon Press, 1984) offer fascinating further insights into the social significance of the old landed élite.
7. Anon. *The Habits of Good Society: A Handbook of Etiquette for Ladies and Gentlemen* (London: James Hogg & Sons, n.d.) 56–7.
8. For British Jewry in this period, see David Feldman, *Englishmen and Jews: Social Relations and Political Culture 1840–1941* (New Haven and London: Yale University Press, 1994).
9. J. H. Newman, 'Philosophy and Religion', Discourse ix in *Discourses on the Scope and Nature of University Education* (Dublin: James Duffy, 1852), 327–8.

CHAPTER 4. TROLLOPE AND POLITICS

1. The authoritative account of English religion in the nineteenth century remains Owen Chadwick's, *The Victorian Church* (2 vols.; London: Black, 1966).
2. For an illuminating insight into old-style clerical kinship and nepotism, see Clive Dewey's study of the Lyall family, *The Passing of*

Barchester: A Real Life Version of Trollope (London: Hambledon Press, 1991).

3. Trollope's distaste for evangelicals may date from his acquaintance with the Revd John William Cunningham, the vicar of Harrow during his boyhood. Cunningham, the author of the pious tract *The Velvet Cushion*, had in 1822 refused to permit the erection of a tablet in memory of Byron's illegitimate daughter, Allegra, on the grounds that (as Trollope later put it) it would 'teach the boys to get bastards'.
4. For an observant and well-argued appreciation of Trollope's political fiction and its relationship to contemporary affairs, see John Halperin, *Trollope and Politics: A Study of the Pallisers and Others* (London: Macmillan, 1977). P. D. Edwards, *Anthony Trollope: His Art and Scope* (St Lucia, Queensland: University of Queensland Press, 1977) is particularly astute about Trollope as a political novelist.
5. The nature of Trollope's party politics has been succinctly and illuminatingly explored in R. F. Foster's pamphlet *Political Novels and Nineteenth-Century History* (Winchester Research Papers in the Humanities; King Alfred's College, Winchester, 1981).
6. A parallel inconsistency in a radical aristocrat is described in the opening chapter of *Marion Fay*.

Select Bibliography

WORKS BY ANTHONY TROLLOPE

Novels

All of Trollope's novels are now available in annotated editions published in the 'World's Classics series by the Oxford University Press. These editions contain generally excellent introductions and bibliographies. The editions in the Penguin Classics series are also to be recommended.

The Macdermots of Ballycloran (3 vols., London: Newby, 1847).
The Kellys and the O'Kellys (3 vols., London: Colburn, 1848).
La Vendée: An Historical Romance (3 vols., London: Colburn, 1850).
The Warden (1 vol., London: Longman, 1855).
Barchester Towers (3 vols., London: Longman, 1857).
The Three Clerks (3 vols., London: Bentley, 1858).
Doctor Thorne (3 vols., London: Chapman & Hall, 1858).
The Bertrams (3 vols., London: Chapman & Hall, 1859).
Castle Richmond (3 vols., London: Chapman & Hall, 1860).
Framley Parsonage (3 vols., London: Smith, Elder, 1861; serialized in the *Cornhill Magazine*, Jan. 1860–June 1861).
Orley Farm (2 vols., London: Chapman & Hall, 1862; serialized in monthly parts, Mar. 1861–Oct. 1862).
The Struggles of Brown, Jones and Robinson (1 vol., London: Smith, Elder, 1870; serialized in the *Cornhill Magazine*, Aug. 1861–Mar. 1862).
Rachel Ray (2 vols., London: Chapman & Hall, 1863).
The Small House at Allington (2 vols., London: Smith, Elder, 1864; serialized in the *Cornhill Magazine*, Sept. 1862–Apr. 1864).
Can You Forgive Her? (2 vols., London: Chapman & Hall, 1864–5; serialized in monthly parts, Jan. 1864–Aug. 1865).
Miss Mackenzie (2 vols., London: Chapman & Hall, 1865).
The Belton Estate (3 vols., London: Chapman & Hall, 1866; serialized in the *Fortnightly Review*, May 1865–Jan. 1866).

Nina Balatka (2 vols., London: Blackwood, 1867); serialized in *Blackwood's Magazine*, July 1866–Jan. 1867).

The Last Chronicle of Barset (2 vols., London: Smith, Elder, 1867; serialized in weekly parts, Dec. 1866–July 1867).

The Claverings (2 vols., London: Smith, Elder, 1867; serialized in the *Cornhill Magazine*, Feb. 1866–May 1867).

Linda Tressel (2 vols., London: Blackwood, 1868; serialized in *Blackwood's Magazine*, Oct. 1867–May 1868).

Phineas Finn (2 vols., London: Virtue, 1869; serialized in *Saint Pauls Magazine*, Oct. 1867–May 1869).

He Knew He Was Right (2 vols., London: Strahan, 1869; serialized in weekly parts, Oct. 1868–May 1869).

The Vicar of Bullhampton (1 vol., London: Bradbury & Evans, 1870; serialized in monthly parts, July 1869–May 1870).

Sir Harry Hotspur of Humblethwaite (1 vol., London: Hurst & Blackett, 1871; serialized in *Macmillan's Magazine*, May–Dec. 1870).

Ralph the Heir (3 vols. London: Hurst & Blackett, 1871; serialized as a supplement to *Saint Pauls Magazine*, Jan. 1870–July 1871 and in monthly parts Jan. 1870–July 1871).

The Golden Lion of Granpere (1 vol., London: Tinsley, 1872; serialized in *Good Words*, Jan.–Aug. 1872).

The Eustace Diamonds (3 vols., London: Chapman & Hall, 1873; serialized in the *Fortnightly Review*, July 1871–Feb. 1873).

Phineas Redux (2 vols., London: Chapman & Hall, 1874; serialized in the *Graphic*, July 1873–Jan. 1874).

Lady Anna (2 vols., London: Chapman & Hall, 1874; serialized in the *Fortnightly Review*, July 1871–Apr. 1874).

Harry Heathcote of Gangoil (1 vol., London: Sampson Low, 1874; Christmas Issue of the *Graphic*, 1873).

The Way We Live Now (2 vols., London: Chapman & Hall, 1875; serialized in monthly parts, Feb. 1874–Sept. 1875).

The Prime Minister (4 vols., London: Chapman & Hall, 1876; serialized in monthly parts, Nov. 1875–June 1876).

The American Senator (3 vols., London: Chapman & Hall, 1877; serialized in *Temple Bar*, May 1876–July 1877).

Is He Popenjoy? (3 vols., London: Chapman & Hall, 1878; serialized in *All the Year Round*, Oct. 1877–July 1878).

An Eye for an Eye (2 vols., London: Chapman & Hall, 1879; serialized in the *Whitehall Review*, Aug. 1878–Feb. 1879).

John Caldigate (3 vols., London: Chapman & Hall, 1879; serialized in *Blackwood's Magazine*, Apr. 1878–June 1879).

Cousin Henry (2 vols., London: Chapman & Hall, 1879; serialized simultaneously in the *Manchester Weekly Times* and the *North British Weekly Mail*, Mar.–May 1879).

The Duke's Children (3 vols., London: Chapman & Hall, 1880; serialized in *All the Year Round*, Oct. 1879–July 1880).

Dr Wortle's School (2 vols., London: Chapman & Hall 1881; serialized in *Blackwood's Magazine*, May–Dec. 1880).

Ayala's Angel (3 vols., London: Chapman & Hall, 1881).

The Fixed Period (2 vols., London: Blackwood, 1882; serialized in *Blackwood's Magazine*, Oct. 1881–Mar. 1882).

Marion Fay (3 vols., London: Chapman & Hall, 1882; serialized in the *Graphic*, Dec. 1881–June 1882).

Kept in the Dark (2 vols., London: Chatto & Windus, 1882; serialized in *Good Words*, May–Dec. 1882).

Mr Scarborough's Family (3 vols., London: Chatto & Windus, 1883; serialized in *All the Year Round*, May 1882–June 1883).

The Land-Leaguers (3 vols., London: Chatto & Windus 1883; serialized in *Life*, Nov. 1882–Oct. 1883).

An Old Man's Love (2 vols., London: Blackwood, 1884).

Collections of Short Stories

Tales of All Countries (London: Chapman & Hall, 1861).

Tales of All Countries: Second Series (London: Chapman & Hall, 1863).

Lotta Schmidt and Other Stories (London: Strahan, 1867).

An Editor's Tales (London: Strahan, 1870).

Why Frau Frohmann Raised her Prices and other Stories (London: Isbister, 1882).

Travel Books

The West Indies and the Spanish Main (London: Chapman & Hall, 1859).

North America (2 vols., London: Chapman & Hall, 1862).

Australia and New Zealand (2 vols., London: Chapman & Hall, 1873).

South Africa (2 vols., London: Chapman & Hall, 1878).

How the 'Mastiffs' Went to Iceland (London: Virtue, 1878).

Other Books

Hunting Sketches (London: Chapman & Hall, 1865).

Travelling Sketches (London: Chapman & Hall, 1866).

Clergymen of the Church of England (London: Chapman & Hall, 1866).

British Sports and Pastimes, ed. by Trollope and includes a preface and the essay 'On Hunting' by him (London: Virtue, 1868).

The Commentaries of Caesar (London: Blackwood, 1870).

Thackeray (London: Macmillan, 1879).

The Life of Cicero (2 vols., London: Chapman & Hall, 1880).

Lord Palmerston (London: Isbister, 1882).

An Autobiography (2 vols., London: Blackwood, 1883).

Since his death further important works by Trollope have been published:

London Tradesmen, ed. Michael Sadleir (London: Constable, 1927).
Four Lectures, ed. Morris L. Parrish (London: Constable, 1938).
The New Zealander, ed. N. John Hall (Oxford: Clarendon Press, 1972).

BIBLIOGRAPHIES

Olmsted, John Charles, and Welch, Jeffrey (eds.) *The Reputation of Trollope: An Annotated Bibliography 1925-1975* (New York: Garland, 1978).

Sadleir, Michael, *Trollope: A Bibliography* (London: Constable, 1928).

LETTERS

The Letters of Anthony Trollope, ed. N. John Hall, with the assistance of Nina Burgis (2 vols., Stanford, Calif.: Stanford University Press, 1983).

BIOGRAPHIES AND BIOGRAPHICAL MATERIAL

Glendenning, Victoria, *Anthony Trollope* (London: Hutchinson, 1992). A very readable account, especially good on Trollope's Irish years.

Hall, N. John, *Trollope: A Biography* (Oxford: Clarendon Press, 1991). The best scholarly life, by the editor of Trollope's letters.

Super, R. H. S., *Trollope in the Post Office* (Ann Arbor, Mich.: University of Michigan Press, 1981). A valuable and detailed account of Trollope's life in the civil service.

Terry, R. C., *Trollope: Interviews and Recollections* (London: Macmillan, 1987). An entertaining and valuable collection.

COMPANIONS AND GUIDES

Escott, T. H. S., *Anthony Trollope: His Work, Associates, and Literary Originals* (London: John Lane, 1913). A prime source of information.

Gerould, Winifred Gregory, and Gerould, James Thayer, *A Guide to Trollope* (Princeton: Princeton University Press, 1948). A somewhat quirky, but still useful book.

Mullen, Richard, with Munson, James, *The Penguin Companion to Trollope*

(London: Penguin Books, 1996). An extremely useful, usable, and intelligent reference book.

Sadleir, Michael, *Trollope: A Commentary* (London: Constable, 1928). A pioneer critical study. Still of great value.

Terry, R. C. (ed.) *Anthony Trollope* (Oxford Author Companions; Oxford: Oxford University Press, forthcoming). This multi-contributor volume will form the standard reference work to Trollope.

CONTEMPORARY CRITICISM OF TROLLOPE

Smalley, Donald (ed.), *Trollope: The Critical Heritage* (London: Routledge & Kegan Paul, 1969). An eminently useful anthology of contemporary criticism of Trollope's works.

CRITICAL AND CONTEXTUAL STUDIES

ap Roberts, Ruth, *Trollope: Artist and Moralist* (London: Chatto & Windus, 1971). An intelligent and challenging study.

Bareham, Tony (ed.), *Anthony Trollope* (London: Vision Press, 1980). A varied collection of critical essays.

Booth, Bradford A., *Anthony Trollope: Aspects of his Life and Art* (London: Edward Hulton, 1958). A pioneer re-evaluation.

Clark, John W., *The Language and Style of Anthony Trollope* (London: Andre Deutsch, 1975). A sound and alert study.

Cockshut, A. O. J., *Anthony Trollope: A Critical Study* (London: Collins, 1955). A forthright appreciation.

Edwards, P. D., *Anthony Trollope, His Art and Scope* (St Lucia, Queensland: University of Queensland Press, 1977). Still one of the very best critical studies.

Hall, N. John, *Trollope and his Illustrators* (London: Macmillan, 1980). A highly informative and beautifully illustrated survey.

Halperin, John, *Trollope and Politics: A Study of the Pallisers and Others* (London: Macmillan, 1977). An important study of 'high' politics in the novels.

——— (ed.) *Trollope: Centenary Essays* (London: Macmillan, 1982). A challenging collection of reconsiderations.

Hamer, Mary, *Writing by Numbers: Trollope's Serial Fictions* (Cambridge: Cambridge University Press, 1987). A significant account of Trollope and novel serialization.

Harvey, Geoffrey, *The Art of Anthony Trollope* (London: Weidenfeld & Nicolson, 1980).

Kincaid, James R., *The Novels of Anthony Trollope* (Oxford: Clarendon

Press, 1977). A fine and observant critical survey.

Letwin, Shirley Robin, *The Gentleman in Trollope: Individuality and Moral Conduct* (London: Macmillan, 1982). An often perceptive socio-critical study.

McMaster, Juliet, *Trollope's Palliser Novels: Theme and Pattern* (London: Macmillan, 1978). An intelligent study of the political fiction.

Markwick, Margaret, *Trollope and Women* (London and Rio Grande: The Hambledon Press, 1997). The most recent account of Trollope's female characters.

Miller, J. Hillis, *Victorian Subjects* (Durham, North Carolina: Duke University Press, 1991). Contains four fine essays dealing with Trollope.

Overton, Bill, *The Unofficial Trollope* (Brighton: Harvester Press, 1982). A sound and observant critical reading.

Polhemus, Robert, *The Changing World of Anthony Trollope* (Berkeley and Los Angeles: University of California Press, 1968). A fine critical survey.

Pollard, Arthur, *Trollope's Political Novels* (Hull: University of Hull, 1968).

——— *Anthony Trollope* (London: Routledge & Kegan Paul, 1978). A direct and thorough, but occasionally pompous book.

Skilton, David, *Anthony Trollope and His Contemporaries: A Study in the Theory and Conventions of Mid-Victorian Fiction* (London: Longman, 1972; reissued London: Macmillan, 1996, with revisions and new preface). A perceptive and singularly intelligent study, placing Trollope in the context of his literary contemporaries.

Sutherland, J. A., *Victorian Novelists and Publishers* (London: University of London, The Athlone Press, 1976). Chapter 6 deals with Trollope's publishing history.

Terry, R. C., *Anthony Trollope: The Artist in Hiding* (London: Macmillan, 1977). A key study of Trollope's art.

Tracy, Robert, *Trollope's Later Novels* (Berkeley and Los Angeles: California: University of California Press, 1978). A major reconsideration of the later fiction.

Wall, Stephen, *Trollope and Character* (London: Faber & Faber, 1988). A perceptively argued appreciation.

Wright, Andrew, *Anthony Trollope: Dream and Art* (London: Macmillan, 1983). An illuminating account of Trollope and imagination.

JOURNAL

Trollopiana, the Journal of the Trollope Society (9a North Street, London SW4 OHN), publishes articles and the texts of the Annual Trollope Lecture.

Index

WRITERS AND THEIR WORK

WRITERS AND THEIR WORK

Title	Author
Alfred Tennyson	*Seamus Perry*
Anita Desai	*Elaine Yee Lin Ho*
Anthony Trollope	*Andrew Sanders*
Byron	*Drummond Bone*
C.S. Lewis	*William Gray*
Charles Dickens	*Rod Mengham*
Chinua Achebe	*Nahem Yousaf*
D.H. Lawrence	*Linda Ruth Williams*
E.M. Forster	*Nicholas Royle*
Franz Kafka	*Michael Wood*
George Eliot	*Josephine McDonagh*
George Orwell	*Douglas Kerr*
Gerard Manley Hopkins	*Daniel Brown*
Harold Pinter	*Mark Taylor-Batty*
Henrik Ibsen, 2nd edition	*Sally Ledger*
Henry James—The Later Writing	*Barbara Hardy*
Jane Austen	*Robert Miles*
John Keats	*Kelvin Everest*
Joseph Conrad	*Cedric Watts*
Leo Tolstoy	*John Bayley*
Oscar Wilde	*Alexandra Warwick*
Paul Scott	*Jacqueline Banerjee*
Percy Bysshe Shelley	*Paul Hamilton*
Philip Larkin, 2nd Edition	*Laurence Lerner*
Robert Browning	*John Woolford*
Rudyard Kipling	*Jan Montefiore*
Samuel Beckett	*Sinéad Mooney*

WRITERS AND THEIR WORK

Title	Author
Samuel Taylor Coleridge	*Stephen Bygrave*
Shashi Deshpande	*Amrita Bhalla*
Sir Walter Scott	*Harriet Harvey Wood*
Stephen Crane	*Kevin J. Hayes*
Swinburne	*Catherine Maxwell*
Sylvia Plath, 2nd edition	*Elisabeth Bronfen*
T.S. Eliot	*Colin MacCabe*
Ted Hughes	*Susan Bassnett*
Thomas Hardy, 2nd Edition	*Peter Widdowson*
V.S. Naipaul	*Suman Gupta*
Victorian Quest Romance	*Robert Fraser*
Virginia Woolf, 2nd Edition	*Laura Marcus*
W.B. Yeasts	*Edward Larrissy*
William Blake	*Steve Vine*
William Golding, 2nd Edition	*Kevin McCarron*
William Makepeace Thackeray	*Richard Salmon*
Wole Soyinka	*Mpalive-Hangson Msiska*